ge

D1033502

Programming JavaScript Applications

Eric Elliott

Beijing · Cambridge · Farnham · Köln · Sebastopol · Tokyo

O'REILLY®

ocn 909538867

Programming JavaScript Applications

by Eric Elliott

Printed in the United States of America.

Published by O'Reilly Media, Inc., 1005 Gravenstein Highway North, Sebastopol, CA 95472.

O'Reilly books may be purchased for educational, business, or sales promotional use. Online editions are also available for most titles (*http://my.safaribooksonline.com*). For more information, contact our corporate/institutional sales department: 800-998-9938 or *corporate@oreilly.com*.

Editors: Simon St. Laurent and Meghan Blanchette	**Indexer:** Lucie Haskins
Production Editor: Kara Ebrahim	**Cover Designer:** Randy Comer
Copyeditor: Eliahu Sussman	**Interior Designer:** David Futato
Proofreader: Amanda Kersey	**Illustrator:** Rebecca Demarest

July 2014:   First Edition

Revision History for the First Edition:

2014-06-25:   First release

See *http://oreilly.com/catalog/errata.csp?isbn=9781491950296* for release details.

ISBN: 978-1-491-95029-6

[LSI]

Table of Contents

Preface

Introduction

There are many books on the web technologies covered in this publication. However, there are precious few on JavaScript that can be recommended to somebody who wants to learn how to build a complete JavaScript application from the ground up. Meanwhile, almost every new tech startup needs knowledgeable JavaScript application developers on staff. This book exists for one purpose: to help you gain the knowledge you need to build complete JavaScript applications that are easy to extend and maintain.

This book is not intended to teach you the basics of JavaScript. Instead, it's designed to build on your existing knowledge and discuss JavaScript features and techniques that will make your code easier to work with over time. Normally, as an application grows, it becomes increasingly difficult to add new features and fix bugs. Your code becomes too rigid and fragile, and even a small change could necessitate a lengthy refactor. If you follow the patterns outlined in this book, your code will remain flexible and resilient. Changes to one piece of code won't negatively impact another.

This book will focus primarily on client-side architecture, although it will also cover server-side topics, such as basic RESTful APIs and Node. The trend is that a great deal of the application logic is getting pushed to the client. It was once the case that the server environment would handle things like templating and communication with vendor services. Now, it's common to deal with both of those jobs inside the browser.

In fact, a modern JavaScript application does almost everything a traditional desktop app would do completely in the browser. Of course, servers are still handy. Server roles frequently include serving static content and dynamically loaded modules, data persistence, action logging, and interfacing with third-party APIs.

We'll cover:

- JavaScript features and best practices for application developers
- Code organization, modularity, and reuse
- Separation of concerns on the client side (MVC, etc.)
- Communicating with servers and APIs
- Designing and programming RESTful APIs with Node.js
- Building, testing, collaboration, deployment, and scaling
- Expanding reach via internationalization

Who This Book Is For

You have some experience with JavaScript; at least a year or two working frequently with the language, but you want to learn more about how you can apply it specifically to developing robust web-scale or enterprise applications.

You know a thing or two about programming, but you have an insatiable thirst to learn more. In particular, you'd like to learn more about how to apply the powerful features that distinguish JavaScript from other languages, such as closures, functional programming, and prototypal inheritance (even if this is the first you've heard of them).

Perhaps you'd also like to learn about how to apply test-driven development (TDD) techniques to your next JavaScript challenge. This book uses tests throughout the code examples. By the time you reach the end, you should be in the habit of thinking about how you'll test the code you write.

Who This Book Is Not For

This book covers a lot of ground quickly. It was not written with the beginner in mind, but if you need clarification, you might find it in *JavaScript: The Good Parts*, by Douglas Crockford (O'Reilly, 2008), *JavaScript: The Definitive Guide*, by David Flannagan (O'Reilly, 2011), or for help with software design patterns, the famous Gang of Four book (GoF), *Design Patterns: Elements of Reusable Object-Oriented Software* (*http://bit.ly/1pwzcUc*), by Erich Gamma, Richard Helm, Ralph Johnson, and John Vlissides (Addison-Wesley, 1994).

Google and Wikipedia can be handy guides to help you through, as well. Wikipedia is a fairly good reference for software design patterns.

If this is your first exposure to JavaScript, you would do well to study some introductory texts and tutorials before you attempt to tackle this book. My favorite is *Eloquent Java-Script* by Marijn Haverbeke (*http://eloquentjavascript.net/*) (No Starch Press, 2011). Be sure to follow that up with *JavaScript: The Good Parts*, and pay special attention to Appendix A so that you can learn from the mistakes made by more experienced Java-Script developers.

Unit Testing

It's difficult to overstate the importance of unit testing. Unit tests are used throughout this book. By the time you reach the end, you should be accustomed to seeing and writing them. As you practice the concepts you read about, start by writing the tests first. You'll get a better understanding of the problem domain, and you'll be forced to think through the design for your solution and the interface you create for it. Designing for unit tests also forces you to keep your code decoupled. The discipline of writing testable, decoupled code will serve you well your entire career.

For a reference on unit tests and code style, see Appendix A.

Conventions Used in This Book

The following typographical conventions are used in this book:

Italic
> Indicates new terms, URLs, email addresses, filenames, and file extensions.

`Constant width`
> Used for program listings, as well as within paragraphs to refer to program elements such as variable or function names, databases, datatypes, environment variables, statements, and keywords.

`Constant width bold`
> Shows commands or other text that should be typed literally by the user.

`Constant width italic`
> Shows text that should be replaced with user-supplied values or by values determined by context.

> This icon signifies a tip, suggestion, or general note.

> This icon indicates a warning or caution.

Safari® Books Online

 Safari Books Online is an on-demand digital library that lets you easily search over 7,500 technology and creative reference books and videos to find the answers you need quickly.

With a subscription, you can read any page and watch any video from our library online. Read books on your cell phone and mobile devices. Access new titles before they are available for print, and get exclusive access to manuscripts in development and post feedback for the authors. Copy and paste code samples, organize your favorites, download chapters, bookmark key sections, create notes, print out pages, and benefit from tons of other time-saving features.

O'Reilly Media has uploaded this book to the Safari Books Online service. To have full digital access to this book and others on similar topics from O'Reilly and other publishers, sign up for free at *http://my.safaribooksonline.com*.

How to Contact Us

Please address comments and questions concerning this book to the publisher:

O'Reilly Media, Inc.
1005 Gravenstein Highway North
Sebastopol, CA 95472
800-998-9938 (in the United States or Canada)
707-829-0515 (international or local)
707-829-0104 (fax)

We have a web page for this book, where we list errata, examples, and any additional information. You can access this page at:

http://bit.ly/programming-jsa

To comment or ask technical questions about this book, send email to:

bookquestions@oreilly.com

For more information about our books, courses, conferences, and news, see our website at *http://www.oreilly.com*.

Find us on Facebook: *http://facebook.com/oreilly*

Follow us on Twitter: *http://twitter.com/oreillymedia*

Watch us on YouTube: *http://www.youtube.com/oreillymedia*

Thanks

Thanks @JS_Cheerleader (*https://twitter.com/JS_Cheerleader*) for encouragement and lots of great JavaScript links.

Thanks to Brendan Eich for his tireless work to drive JavaScript and the web forward. Thanks to the team at O'Reilly. To Simon St. Laurent, who immediately recognized the value of the book and provided a lot of encouragement along the way. To Brian McDonald, whose valuable feedback made this a much better book. To Meghan Blanchette for keeping the momentum alive. Thanks to the following individuals for their great technical feedback:

- César Andreu
- James Halliday (Substack)
- Hugh Jackson
- Ramsey Lawson
- Shelley Powers
- Kyle Simpson
- Kevin Western

A special thank you to the people who have contributed to the open source projects written for this book, and to all of the open source contributors who make programming JavaScript applications a much better experience every single day. As software developers, we are all standing on the shoulders of giants.

## CHAPTER 1

The JavaScript Revolution

JavaScript is arguably the most important programming language on earth. Once thought of as a toy, JavaScript is now the most widely deployed programming language in history. Almost everyone with a computer or a smartphone has all the tools they need to execute JavaScript programs and to create their own. All you need is a browser and a text editor.

JavaScript, HTML, and CSS have become so prevalent that many operating systems have adopted the open web standards as the presentation layer for native apps, including Windows 8 (*http://bit.ly/1pFDDx2*), Firefox OS (*http://mzl.la/1oO2i1J*), Gnome (*http://bit.ly/1pFBnFV*), and Google's Chrome OS (*http://www.chromium.org/chromium-os*). Additionally, the iPhone and Android mobile devices support web views that allow them to incorporate JavaScript and HTML5 functionality into native applications.

JavaScript is also moving into the hardware world. Projects like Arduino (*http://bit.ly/1iY0ceO*), Tessel (*http://tessel.io/*), Espruino (*http://www.espruino.com/*), and Node-Bots (*http://nodebots.io/*) foreshadow a time in the near future where JavaScript could be a common language for embedded systems and robotics.

Creating a JavaScript program is as simple as editing a text file and opening it in the browser. There are no complex development environments to download and install, and no complex IDE to learn. JavaScript is easy to learn, too. The basic syntax is immediately familiar to any programmer who has been exposed to the C family syntax. No other language can boast a barrier to entry as low as JavaScript's.

That low barrier to entry is probably the main reason that JavaScript was once widely (perhaps rightly) shunned as a toy. It was mainly used to create UI effects in the browser. That situation has changed.

For a long time, there was no way to save data with JavaScript. If you wanted data to persist, you had to submit a form to a web server and wait for a page refresh. That hindered the process of creating responsive and dynamic web applications. However, in 2000, Microsoft started shipping Ajax technology in Internet Explorer. Soon after, other browsers added support for the XMLHttpRequest object.

In 2004, Google launched Gmail. Initially applauded because it promised users nearly infinite storage for their email, Gmail also brought a major revolution. Gone were the page refreshes. Under the hood, Gmail was taking advantage of the new Ajax technology, creating a single-page, fast, and responsive web application that would forever change the way that web applications are designed.

Since that time, web developers have produced nearly every type of application, including full-blown, cloud-based office suites (see Zoho.com), social APIs like Facebook's JavaScript SDK, and even graphically intensive video games.

All of this is serving to prove Atwood's Law (*http://bit.ly/1pFCjtR*): "Any application that can be written in JavaScript, will eventually be written in JavaScript."

Advantages of JavaScript

JavaScript didn't just luck into its position as the dominant client-side language on the Web. It is actually very well suited to be the language that took over the world. It is one of the most advanced and expressive programming languages developed to date. The following sections outline some of the features you may or may not be familiar with.

Performance

Just-in-time compiling: in modern browsers, most JavaScript is compiled, highly optimized, and executed like native code, so runtime performance is close to that of software written in C or C++. Of course, there is still the overhead of garbage collection and dynamic binding, so it is possible to do certain things faster; however, the difference is generally not worth sweating over until you've optimized everything else. With Node.js (*http://nodejs.com/*) (a high-performance, evented, server-side JavaScript environment built on Google's highly optimized V8 JavaScript engine), JavaScript apps are event driven and nonblocking, which generally more than makes up for the code execution difference between JavaScript and less dynamic languages.

Objects

JavaScript has very rich object-oriented (OO) features. The *JSON* (JavaScript Object Notation) standard used in nearly all modern web applications for both communication and data persistence is a subset of JavaScript's excellent object-literal notation.

JavaScript uses a *prototypal inheritance* model. Instead of classes, you have object prototypes. New objects automatically inherit methods and attributes of their parent object through the *prototype chain*. It's possible to modify an object's prototype at any time, making JavaScript a very flexible, dynamic language.

Prototypal OO is so much more flexible than classical inheritance that it's possible to mimic Java's class-based OO and inheritance models in JavaScript virtually feature for feature, and in most cases, with less code. The reverse is not true.

Contrary to common belief, JavaScript supports features like encapsulation, polymorphism, multiple inheritance, and composition. You'll learn more about these topics in Chapter 3.

Syntax

The JavaScript syntax should be immediately familiar to anybody who has experience with C-family languages, such as C++, Java, C#, and PHP. Part of JavaScript's popularity is due to its familiarity, though it's important to understand that JavaScript behaves very differently from all of these under the hood.

JavaScript's object-literal syntax is so simple, flexible, and concise, it was adapted to become the dominant standard for client/server communication in the form of JSON, which is more compact and flexible than the XML that it replaced.

First-Class Functions

In JavaScript, objects are not a tacked-on afterthought. Nearly everything in JavaScript is an object, including functions. Because of that feature, functions can be used anywhere you might use a variable, including the parameters in function calls. That feature is often used to define anonymous callback functions for asynchronous operations, or to create *higher order functions* (functions that take other functions as parameters, return a function, or both). Higher-order functions are used in the *functional programming* style to abstract away commonly repeated coding patterns, such as iteration loops or other instruction sets that differ mostly in the variables or data they consume.

Good examples of functional programing include functions like .map(), .reduce(), and .forEach(). The Underscore.js (*http://bit.ly/1pFECwY*) library contains many useful functional utilities. For simplicity, we'll be making use of Underscore.js in this book.

Events

Inside the browser, everything runs in an event loop. JavaScript coders quickly learn to think in terms of event handlers, and as a result, code from experienced JavaScript developers tends to be well organized and efficient. Operations that might block processing in other languages happen concurrently in JavaScript.

If you click something, you want something to happen instantly. That impatience has led to wonderful advancements in UI design, such as Google Instant and the groundbreaking address lookup on The Wilderness Downtown (*http://thewildernessdown town.com/*). ("The Wilderness Downtown" is an interactive short film by Chris Milk set to the Arcade Fire song, "We Used To Wait." It was built entirely with the latest open web technologies.) Such functionality is powered by Ajax calls that do their thing in the background without slowing down the UI.

Reusability

JavaScript code, by virtue of its ubiquity, is the most portable, reusable code around. What other language lets you write the same code that runs natively on both the client and the server? (See "Getting Started with Node and Express" on page 125 to learn about an event-driven JavaScript environment that is revolutionizing server-side development.)

JavaScript can be modular and encapsulated, and it is common to see scripts written by six different teams of developers who have never communicated working in harmony on the same page.

The Net Result

JavaScript developers are at the heart of what may be the single biggest revolution in the history of computing: the dawn of the realtime web. Messages pass back and forth across the net, in some cases with each keystroke, or every move of the mouse. We're writing applications that put desktop application UI's to shame. Modern JavaScript applications are the most responsive, most socially engaging applications ever written—and if you don't know JavaScript yet, you're missing the boat. It's time to get on board, before you get left behind.

Anatomy of a Typical Modern JavaScript App

While every app is unique, most share some common concerns, such as hosting infrastructure, resource management, presentation, and UI behaviors. This section covers where these various elements typically live in the application and the common mechanisms that allow them to communicate.

Infrastructure

Infrastructure can come in many flavors and have lots of different caching mechanisms. Generally, it consists of (back to front):

- A data store
- A virtual private network (VPN) or firewall (to protect the data store from unauthorized access)
- A black box JSON RESTful Web Service Layer
- Various third-party APIs

- An app server/content management system (CMS) to route requests and deliver pages to the client
- A static content deliver network (CDN) for cached files (like images, JavaScript, CSS, and client-side templates)
- The client (browser)

To see how these generally fit together, see Figure 1-1.

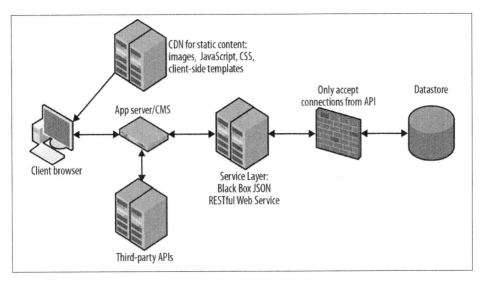

Figure 1-1. Infrastructure

Most of these components are self explanatory, but there are some important points that you should be aware of concerning the storage and communication of application data.

The data store is just like it sounds: a place to store your application data. This is commonly a relational database management system (RDBMS) with a Structured Query Language (SQL) API, but the popularity of NoSQL solutions is on the rise. In the future, it's likely that many applications will use a combination of both.

JSON: Data Storage and Communication

JavaScript Object Notation (JSON) is an open standard developed by Douglas Crockford that specifies a subset of the native JavaScript object-literal syntax for use in data representation, communication, and storage.

Prior to the JSON specification, most client-server communications were being delivered in much more verbose XML snippets. JavaScript developers often work with JSON web services and frequently define internal data using JSON syntax.

Take this example message, describing a collection of books:

```
[
    {
        "title" : "JavaScript: The Good Parts",
        "author" : "Douglas Crockford",
        "ISBN" : "0596517742"
    },
    {
        "title" : "JavaScript Patterns",
        "author" : "Stoyan Stefanov",
        "ISBN" : "0596806752"
    }
]
```

As you can see, this format is nearly identical to JavaScript's object-literal syntax, with a couple important differences:

- All attributes names and string values must be enclosed in double quotes. Other values may appear in their literal form.
- JSON records cannot contain circular references.
- JSON cannot contain functions.

NoSQL Data Stores

Prior to the advent of Extensible Markup Language (XML) and JSON data stores, nearly all web services were backed by RDBMS. An RDBMS stores discrete data points in tables and groups data output using table lookups in response to SQL queries.

NoSQL data stores, in contrast, store entire records in documents or document snippets without resorting to table-based structured storage. Document-oriented data stores commonly store data in XML format, while object-oriented data stores commonly employ the JSON format. The latter are particularly well suited to web application development, because JSON is the format you use to communicate natively in JavaScript.

Examples of popular JSON-based NoSQL data stores include MongoDB (*http:// www.mongodb.org/*) and CouchDB (*http://couchdb.apache.org/*). Despite the recent popularity of NoSQL, it is still common to find modern JavaScript applications backed by MySQL and similar RDBMSs.

RESTful JSON Web Services

Representational State Transfer (REST) is a client-server communication architecture that creates a separation of concerns between data resources and user interfaces (or other data resource consumers, such as data analysis tools and aggregators). Services that implement REST are referred to as RESTful. The server manages data resources (such as user records). It does not implement the user interface (look and feel). Clients are free to implement the UI (or not) in whatever manner or language is desired. REST architecture does not address how user interfaces are implemented. It only deals with maintaining application state between the client and the server.

RESTful web services use HTTP verbs to tell the server what action the client intends. The actions supported are:

- Create a new entry in the resource collection: HTTP POST.
- Retrieve a resource representation: HTTP GET verb.
- Update (replace) the resource: HTTP PUT.
- Delete a resource: HTTP DELETE.

This might look familiar if you're familiar with CRUD (create, retrieve, update, delete). Just remember that in the REST mapping, update really means *replace*.

Figure 1-2 shows a typical state transfer flow.

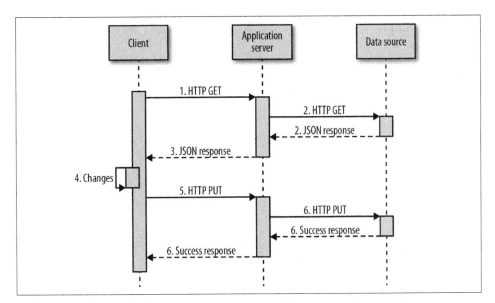

Figure 1-2. REST sequence

1. The client requests data from the server with an HTTP GET request to the resource *uniform resource indicator* (URI). Each resource on the server has a unique URI.

2. The server retrieves the data (typically from a database or cache) and packages it into a convenient representation for the client.

3. Data is returned in the form of a document. Those documents are commonly text strings containing JSON encoded objects, but REST is agnostic about how you package your data. It's also common to see XML-based RESTful services. Most new services default to JSON formatted data, and many support both XML and JSON.

4. The client manipulates the data representation.

5. The client makes a call to the same endpoint URI with a PUT, sending back the manipulated data.

6. The resource data on the server is replaced by the data in the PUT request.

It's common to be confused about whether to use PUT or POST to change a resource. REST eases that confusion. PUT is used if the client is capable of generating its own safe IDs. Otherwise, a POST request is always made on a collection to create a new resource. In this case, the server generates the ID and returns it to the client.

For example, you might create a new user by hitting /users/ with a POST request, at which point the server will generate a unique ID that you can use to access the new resource at /users/userid. The server will return a new user representation with its own unique URI. You shouldn't modify an existing resource with POST; you can add only children to it.

Use PUT to change the user's display name by hitting /users/userid with the updated user record. Note that this will completely replace the user record, so make sure that the representation you PUT contains everything you want it to contain.

You can learn more about working with REST in Chapter 8.

## CHAPTER 2

Functions

Functions are the building blocks of applications. They are particularly important in JavaScript because JavaScript supports first-class functions, functions as objects, run-time function definition, and so on. JavaScript's features allow you to use functions in ways that you may not be familiar with. It's important to have a thorough understanding of how functions work in JavaScript so you can leverage them to full advantage in your applications. By the end of this chapter, you should see functions in a whole new light.

Here are some guidelines that will help you write better functions:

Don't Repeat Yourself (DRY)
> Good programmers are both lazy and very productive. They express a lot of functionality in very little code. Once you have established a pattern for something that gets repeated again in the code, it's time to write a function, object, or module that encapsulates that pattern so that it can be easily reused.
>
> Doing so also quarantines that functionality to a single spot in the code base, so that if you later find something wrong with the code or the algorithm, you only have to fix it in one place.
>
> Writing a reusable function also forces you to isolate the pattern from the problem, which helps you keep related functionality grouped together.

Do One Thing (DOT)
> Each function should do only one thing, and do that one thing as well as it can. Following this principle will make your function more reusable, more readable, and easier to debug.

Keep It Simple Stupid (KISS)
> Programmers are often tempted to come up with clever solutions to problems. That's a good thing, of course, but sometimes programmers are *too clever,* and the

solutions are cryptic. This tends to happen when a single line of code is used to accomplish more than a single atomic goal.

Less Is More

In order to aid readability and reduce the temptation to do more than one thing, functions should be as short as possible: Just enough code to do the one thing they were made to do, and no more. In most cases, functions should be just a handful of lines long. If they run much longer, consider breaking out subtasks and data into separate functions and objects.

Minimize Side Effects

There are two classes of bugs that are extremely common and easily avoidable. The first is syntax errors (covered in "Code Quality" on page 209). The second is unintentional side effects.

Unintentional side effects are the bane of code reuse. They occur when multiple functions depend on and manipulate the values of the same variables or object properties. In this situation, it becomes much more difficult to refactor code, because your functions assume too much about the state of the program. For example, imagine your app includes a shopping cart, and your users can save cart contents between sessions.

Now the user wants to change the order *for the current session, only*:

```
test('Order WITH unintentional side effect.', function () {
  var cartProto = {
      items: [],

      addItem: function addItem(item) {
        this.items.push(item);
      }
    },

    createCart = function (items) {
      var cart = Object.create(cartProto);
      cart.items = items;
      return cart;
    },

    // Load cart with stored items.
    savedCart = createCart(["apple", "pear", "orange"]),

    session = {
      get: function get() {
        return this.cart;
      },

      // Grab the saved cart.
      cart: createCart(savedCart.items)
```

```
    };

    // addItem gets triggered by an event handler somewhere:
    session.cart.addItem('grapefruit');

    ok(session.cart.items.indexOf('grapefruit')
      !== -1, 'Passes: Session cart has grapefruit.');

    ok(savedCart.items.indexOf('grapefruit') === -1,
      'Fails: The stored cart is unchanged.');
});
```

Sadly, when the user adds or removes items from his session cart, those changes will destroy the settings for the stored cart that he wants to use later. The trouble with this code is here:

```
createCart = function (items) {
  var cart = Object.create(cartProto);
  cart.items = items;
  return cart;
},
```

At this point, `cart.items` is a reference to the prototype `items` attribute. This is improved with one small change to the code:

```
cart.items = Object.create(items);
```

Now the new cart will have its own copy of the item data, so changes will not be destructive to `storedCart`.

The best way to ensure that your `program` contains few unintentional side effects is to avoid them in your *functions*. If your function operates on outside variables, return a *copy* instead of the original.

A *pure function* has no side effects. It does not alter existing variables or program state in any way, and always returns the same value given the same inputs.

Wherever possible, make sure that your functions don't change anything outside the function itself. Return amended copies rather than originals. Note that you can still alter program state. REST works this way: you get a *copy* of the data resource (called a *representation*), manipulate it, and send the copy back to the server. Sometimes performance implications make this advice impractical, but it's helpful to consider the possibility of using pure functions.

Writing most of your functions in a similar fashion can help you separate concerns and reduce code duplication. For example, if you need to implement data validation months after you wrote the original code and you have a single function that is responsible for writing data to your data resource, it will be trivial to add the needed validation. If hundreds of functions throughout the codebase are accessing the data directly, it will be a much more difficult task.

Keeping things isolated in this way can also enhance your ability to implement state management. If the functions that manipulate data don't have to worry about the state of the program and account for side effects created by other functions, they can do their job with much less code. All they have to know how to do is the *one task* they were designed to do.

Likewise, the only functions that should be manipulating the DOM should be the methods dedicated to DOM manipulation, such as a view's `.render()` method or a DOM plug-in.

Function Definition

There are several ways to define functions in JavaScript. Each has its own advantages and disadvantages:

```
function foo() {

  /* Warning: arguments.callee is deprecated.
     Use with caution. Used here strictly for
     illustration. */

  return arguments.callee;
}

foo(); //=> [Function: foo]
```

In this code, `foo()` is a *function declaration*. As mentioned in "Hoisting" on page 22, it's important to be aware that you can't declare a function conditionally. For example, the following code will fail:

```
var score = 6;

if (score > 5) {
  function grade() {
    return 'pass';
  }
} else {
  function grade() {
    return 'fail';
  }
}

module('Pass or Fail');

test('Conditional function declaration.', function () {

  // Firefox: Pass
  // Chrome, Safari, IE, Opera: Fail
  equal(grade(), 'pass',
```

```
        'Grade should pass.');
    });
```

What's worse, this pattern fails inconsistently across browsers. It's best to avoid conditional function declarations entirely. For more detail, refer to "Hoisting" on page 22.

Function declaration tends to encourage large piles of loosely related functions to grow in your module, with no real hints about what goes where, whether it's public or private, or how the functions work together:

```
var bar = function () {
    return arguments.callee;
};

bar(); //=> [Function] (Note: It's anonymous.)
```

The `bar()` example assigns a function body to the variable, `bar`. This implementation is called a *function expression*.

The advantage of function expressions is you can assign functions to variables the same way you would assign values to variables. You can count on function expressions to follow your application logic reliably. If you want to do a conditional assignment, it will work as expected.

The disadvantage is function expressions create *anonymous functions* unless you explicitly provide a name. Anonymous functions are used in JavaScript frequently—with reckless abandon, perhaps. Imagine that you've declared all of your functions this way, and you have a pile of functions that call functions that call even more functions. This is a common scenario in a well-architected, event-driven application. Now imagine that you're 12 function calls deep and something goes wrong. You need to debug and view your call stack, but it looks something like this:

```
(Anonymous function)
(Anonymous function)
(Anonymous function)
(Anonymous function)
(Anonymous function)
(Anonymous function)
(Anonymous function)
(Anonymous function)
(Anonymous function)
(Anonymous function)
(Anonymous function)
(Anonymous function)
```

Obviously, this is not very helpful:

```
var baz = {
    f: function () {
        return arguments.callee;
    }
};
```

```
baz.f(); // => [Function] (Note: Also anonymous.)
```

The `baz` example exhibits the same behavior. It's another anonymous function assigned to a property in an object literal. Function expressions assigned to object literals are sometimes called *method literals*. Methods are functions attached to objects.

The advantage is that method literals make it very easy to group related functions using object literals. For example, say you have a group of functions that control the state of a lightbulb:

```
var lightBulbAPI = {
    toggle: function () {},
    getState: function () {},
    off: function () {},
    on: function () {},
    blink: function () {}
};
```

You gain a lot when you group related functions together. Your code is more organized and readable. Code in context is easier to understand and maintain.

Another advantage is that you can more easily rearrange code if you notice that your module is growing too large. For example, if your smart-house module is too bulky with APIs for lightbulbs, TV, music, and the garage door, and they're all grouped like this, it's much easier to split them into individual modules in separate files.

 Do not use the `Function()` constructor to declare a function. Passing it a string is equivalent to passing a string to `eval()`. It comes with the same drawbacks and security implications discussed in Chapter 2.

Named Function Expressions

As you can see, all of the function definition techniques have weaknesses, but it's possible to get the benefits of code organization and conditional function definition without littering your stack traces with anonymous functions. Let's take another look at the lightbulb API:

```
var lightbulbAPI = {
    toggle: function toggle() {},
    getState: function getState() {},
    off: function off() {},
    on: function on() {},
    blink: function blink() {}
};
```

Named function expressions are like anonymous function expressions in every way, except that they have a name that you can use from inside the function (for recursion). That name also conveniently appears in the function call stack.

As with anonymous function expressions, you can use them anywhere you would use a variable—not just inside method literals. Named function expressions are *not* the same as function declarations. Unlike function declarations, the name you assign is only available from within the function (covered in more detail in "Function Scope" on page 22). From outside the function, you must access the function through the variable it's assigned to or the parameter it's passed in on:

```
test('Named function expressions.', function () {
  var a = function x () {
    ok(x, 'x() is usable inside the function.');
  };

  a();

  try {
    x(); // Error
  } catch (e) {
    ok(true, 'x() is undefined outside the function.');
  }
});
```

Internet Explorer 8 and older treat named function expressions like function declarations, so be careful that the names you choose won't collide with the names of other functions or variables in the same scope. This bug is fixed in IE9. All other major browsers treat named function expressions correctly.

If you name your function expressions the same as the variable you assign them to and declare all of your variables at the top of your function, this will rarely be a problem.

```
test('Function Scope', function () {
  var testDeclaration = false,
    foo;

  // This function gets erroneously overridden in IE8.
  function bar(arg1, bleed) {
    if (bleed) {

      ok(false,
        'Declaration bar() should NOT be callable from'
        + ' inside the expression.');

    } else {
```

```
        ok(true,
            'Declaration bar() should be called outside the'
            + ' expression.');

    }
    testDeclaration = true;
}

foo = function bar(declaration, recurse) {
    if (recurse) {

        ok(true,
            'Expression bar() should support scope safe'
            + ' recursion');

    } else if (declaration === true) {

        ok(true,
            'Expression bar() should be callable via foo()');
            bar(false, true);

    } else {

        // Fails in IE8 and older
        ok(false,
        'Expression bar() should NOT be callable outside'
        + ' the expression');

    }
};

bar();
foo(true);

// Fails in IE8 and older
ok(testDeclaration,
    'The bar() declaration should NOT get overridden by'
    + ' the expression bar()');
});
```

Lambdas

A *lambda* is a function that is used as data. As such, it can be used the same way any other expression can: as a parameter for another function, the return value of a function, or anywhere you might use a literal value.

For example:

```
var sum = function sum() {
    var result = 0;

    [5, 5, 5].forEach(function addTo(number) { result += number; });
```

```
    return result;
};

test('Lambdas.', function () {
  equal(sum(), 15,
    'result should be 15.');
});
```

The `.addTo()` function passed into `.forEach()` is a lambda. The `.forEach()` method calls `.addTo()` for each number in the array. Note that `.addTo()` has access to the `result` variable from the containing function scope's closure (covered in more detail in "Closures" on page 25). The `.forEach()` method is one of several *functional enumerators* added to JavaScript in the ECMAScript 5 specification. More detail on that can be found in "Functional Programming" on page 36.

In JavaScript, lambdas are commonly used to:

- Perform operations on the other arguments passed in (as demonstrated earlier).
- Attach event handlers for DOM interactions.
- Pass in a *callback function* to be executed when the current function is complete.
- Wrap existing functions with additional functionality (often used to implement cross-cutting concerns, such as logging). A function that adds functionality to another function is called a *function decorator.*
- Take a function that requires multiple parameters, and return a function that requires fewer parameters—for example, by fixing one or more of the parameters to specific values. (See "Partial Application and Currying" on page 40.)
- Return a function from another function. For example, you might have a function that takes an argument and returns a curried function that applies that argument in a predetermined calculation.

Lambdas are frequently confused with anonymous functions, closures, first-class functions, and higher order functions. The concepts are all similar, but they mean different things.

Some languages use a character (such as " or "), or the keyword `lambda` to denote lambdas and leave off the function name. Don't let that fool you. Function anonymity is merely syntactical sugar for lambdas, designed to make them less verbose and easier to work with. The important point is that lambdas are treated like data that can be passed around as inputs and outputs between other functions, regardless of whether or not they are named.

It is common to confuse the words "closure" and "lambda" as synonyms. That is not accurate. Not all lambdas are closures, and not all closures are lambdas. A closure is created when a function references data that is contained outside the function scope. A lambda is a function that is used as a value (assigned to a variable or passed between functions). Some languages support lambdas but do not support closures.

All functions in JavaScript are first class, meaning that you can use them anywhere you would use a value, so it's possible to create a first-class function that is not also a lambda. You can pass any function as data, but when we talk about lambdas in JavaScript, we're talking about actually taking advantage of that capability by treating the function like a value.

Higher-order functions are functions that consume or return functions as data. Lambdas get passed to and/or returned from higher order functions, and a function might be both a lambda and a higher order function, but not all higher order functions are lambdas.

 If a function is used as an argument or return value, it's a lambda.

Immediately Invoked Function Expressions

It's possible in JavaScript to immediately invoke a function as soon as it's defined. A popular name for the technique is a *self-invoked anonymous function*. That name is not accurate because it incorrectly implies that the function is recursive. Ben Alman posted a better suggestion on his blog (*http://bit.ly/i-ife*): *Immediately Invoked Function Expression* (IIFE, pronounced *"iffy"*). The name is a lot more fun to say in the abbreviated form, and clearly describes what it is. Thankfully, the name IIFE seems to be taking root.

This technique is often used to create a new scope to encapsulate modules. jQuery uses IIFEs to isolate its variables from the global scope. Before the IIFE became popular, a common technique was to assign names to the object prototype:

```
var Lightbulb = function () {
    this.isOn = false;
  },
  lightbulb = new Lightbulb();

Lightbulb.prototype.toggle = function () {
  this.isOn = !this.isOn;
  return this.isOn;
};

Lightbulb.prototype.getState = function getState() {
  // Implementation...
};

Lightbulb.prototype.off = function off() {
```

```
  // Implementation...
};

Lightbulb.prototype.on = function on() {
  // Implementation...
};

Lightbulb.prototype.blink = function blink() {
  // Implementation...
};

test('Prototypes without IIFE.', function () {
  equal(lightbulb.toggle(), true, 'Lightbulb turns on.');
  equal(lightbulb.toggle(), false, 'Lightbulb turns off.');
});
```

As you can see, this method leads to a lot of repetition, as you have to specifically address `lightbulb.prototype` for every property definition. The IIFE lets you encapsulate scope, so you can assign to regular variables, instead of just the prototype. This gives you more flexibility and the ability to hide state inside the function closure:

```
(function () {
  var isOn = false,
    toggle = function toggle() {
      isOn = !isOn;
      return isOn;
    },
    getState = function getState() {
      // Implementation...
    },
    off = function off() {
      // Implementation...
    },
    on = function on() {
      // Implementation...
    },
    blink = function blink() {
      // Implementation...
    },

    lightbulb = {
      toggle: toggle,
      getState: getState,
      off: off,
      on: on,
      blink: blink
    };

  test('Prototypes with IIFE.', function () {
    equal(lightbulb.toggle(), true,
      'Lightbulb turns on.');
    equal(lightbulb.toggle(), false,
```

```
        'Lightbulb turns off.');
    });
  }());
```

Method Context

Functions are invoked by appending parentheses to the end of the function reference. For these examples, we'll use a slightly altered `highPass()` function:

```
function highPass(number, cutoff) {
    cutoff = cutoff || this.cutoff;
    return (number >= cutoff);
}

var filter1 = {
    highPass: highPass,
    cutoff: 5
  },
  filter2 = {
    // No highPass here!
    cutoff: 3
  };
```

The `highPass()` function takes one required parameter for the `number` to be tested and one optional parameter for the `cutoff`. If the optional parameter is not supplied, the function assumes that it is being called as a method of a valid filter object and uses the `cutoff` property of the object instead.

Function invocation is simple:

```
test('Invoking a function.', function () {
  var result = highPass(6, 5);

  equal(result, true,
    '6 > 5 should be true.');
});
```

Unless you use *method invocation* (*dot notation* or *square bracket notation*), `this` generally refers to the global object. Assignments to properties on `this` will pollute the global namespace. It's better to make sure you have a valid object before trying to use `this` in your function if you expect it might be invoked on its own.

Method invocation applies the function to the object to which it is attached. It takes the form `object.methodName()` (dot notation) or `object['methodName']()` (square bracket notation):

```
test('Invoking a method.', function () {
  var result1 = filter1.highPass(3),
    result2 = highPass.call(filter2, 3),
```

```
    result3 = filter1.highPass(6);

  equal(result1, false,
    '3 >= filter1.cutoff should be false.');

  equal(result2, true,
    '3 >= filter2.cutoff should be true.');

  equal(result3, true,
    '6 >= filter1.cutoff should be true.');
});
```

When you invoke a method with dot notation, you have access to the object's properties using this. The number parameter is compared to filter1.cutoff. The method returns false because 3 is less than the value stored in this.cutoff, which refers to filter1.cutoff. Remember, this refers to the object that the method is called on.

In the second example, the call method (inherited from Function.prototype) delegates to the method on filter2 instead. Because filter2.cutoff is 3 instead of 5, the same test passes this time.

To clarify, the .call() method shared by all functions allows you to call any method or function on any object. In other words, it sets this inside the method to refer to the object of your choosing. The signature is:

```
someMethod.call(context, argument1, argument2, ...);
```

Here, context is the object you want this to refer to. If you need to pass an array of arguments, use .apply() instead:

```
someMethod.apply(context, someArray);
```

Function.prototype.bind()

As useful as .call() and .apply() can be, they have one serious drawback: they impermanently bind the context to the target method. You have to remember to use them every time you invoke the method, and you have to have access to the context object in scope. That's not always easy, particularly in event handlers.

The .bind() method is used to permanently set the value of this inside the target function to the passed in context object. The .bind() method is a recent addition to the language. It was first popularized by Prototype and adopted in many other libraries and was standardized in ECMAScript 5. If you want to use it in older browsers, you'll need to shim it or use one of many available library implementations.

Let's take a look at a common use case for .bind()—an event handler:

```
var lightbulb = {
    toggle: function toggle() {
      this.isOn = !this.isOn;
      return this.isOn;
```

```
    },
      isOn: false
    },
    toggle = lightbulb.toggle,
    lightswitch = document.getElementById('lightswitch');

  lightswitch = document.getElementById('lightswitch');
  lightswitch.addEventListener('click',
    lightbulb.toggle, false);
```

Glancing over this code, it looks simple enough. An event listener gets attached to the lightswitch DOM with `.addEventListener()`. There's just one problem: this code will fail because the context inside an event listener is not the object that the method was assigned to at design time. Instead, it's a reference to the element that was clicked.

Even after you click the switch element, `lightbulb.isOn` will be `false`. You can fix this mess with `.bind()`. You only need to alter the toggle assignment:

```
    toggle = lightbulb.toggle.bind(lightbulb);
```

Now, when the user clicks the lightswitch, the lightbulb will turn on or off as expected.

Function Scope

Variable scope is the section of code in which the identifier refers to the expected value. Outside a variable's scope, the variable is undefined or replaced by another variable with the same name. Most C-family languages have *block scope*, meaning that you can create blocks arbitrarily to contain variables. The `var` keyword is not block scoped. This is a common source of confusion among people who are new to JavaScript but familiar with other languages.

`var` uses *function scope* instead. Block scope will be available using the `let` keyword in ES6. It is already implemented in several browsers, but it may be some time before you can safely use it if you need wide cross-browser support.

 The desire to use block scope can be a good code smell that indicates that it may be time to break a function into smaller pieces in order to encourage readability, organization, and code reuse. It's a good idea to keep functions small.

Hoisting

Hoisting is the word most commonly used to describe the illusion that all variable declarations are "hoisted" to the top of the containing function. Technically, that's not exactly how it happens, but the effect is the same.

JavaScript builds its execution environment in two passes. The declaration pass sets up the runtime environment, where it scans for all variable and function declarations and creates the identifiers. The second pass is the execution pass. After the first pass, all declared functions are available, but variables are still undefined. Consider this code:

```
var x = 1;

(function () {
  console.log(x);
  var x = 2;
}());
```

If you guessed that the value of x at the `console.log()` statement is 1, you're not alone. This is a common source of bugs in JavaScript. In the first pass, the function declarations occur, and x is undefined in both the inner and outer scope. When it gets to the con sole.log() statement in the execution pass, the inner scoped x has been declared, but is still undefined, because it hasn't hit the initialization in the next statement yet. In effect, this is how JavaScript interprets the code:

```
var x = 1;

(function () {
  var x; // Declaration is hoisted and x is undefined.
  console.log(x);
  x = 2; // Initialization is still down here.
}());
```

Functions behave a little differently. Both the identifier number and the function body are hoisted, whereas the value 2 was not hoisted along with x:

```
test('Function declaration hoisting', function () {
  function number() {
    return 1;
  }

  (function () {
    equal(number(), 2, 'Inner scope wins.');

    function number() {
      return 2;
    }
  }());

  equal(number(), 1, 'Outer scope still works.');
});
```

This code is equivalent to:

```
test('Function declaration hoisted.', function () {
  function number() {
    return 1;
  }
```

```
(function () {
  function number() {
    return 2;
  }

  equal(number(), 2, 'Inner scope wins.');
}());

equal(number(), 1, 'Outer scope still works.');
});
```

Function expressions do not share this behavior, because they do not declare a function. Instead, they declare a variable and are subject to the same variable-hoisting behavior:

```
test('Function expression hoisting', function () {
  function number() {
    return 1;
  }

  (function () {
    try {
      number();
    } catch (e) {
      ok(true, 'number() is undefined.');
    }

    var number = function number() {
      return 2;
    }

    equal(number(), 2, 'number() is defined now.');
  }());

  equal(number(), 1, 'Outer scope still works.');
});
```

In the function expression example, the number variable is hoisted, but the function body is *not hoisted*, because it is a named function expression, not a function declaration. The value of number is not defined until runtime. This code is equivalent to:

```
test('Function Expression Hoisted', function () {
  function number() {
    return 1;
  }

  (function () {
    var number; // Declaration initialized to undefined.

    try {
      number();
    } catch (e) {
      ok(true, 'number() is undefined.');
```

```
      }

    number = function number() {
      return 2;
    }

    equal(number(), 2, 'number() is defined now.');
  }());

  equal(number(), 1, 'Outer scope still works.');
});
```

 If you declare all of your variables at the top of your function, and define your functions before you try to use them, you'll never need to worry about any of this. This practice can substantially reduce scope-related bugs.

Closures

Closures are critical to successful application development.

In a nutshell, a *closure* stores function state, even after the function has returned. To create a closure, simply define a function inside another function and expose it. To expose a function, return it or pass it to another function. The inner function will have access to the variables declared in the outer function. This technique is commonly used to give objects data privacy.

Because the closure variables in the outer function are only in scope within the containing function, you can't get at the data except through its *privileged methods*. In other languages, a privileged method is an exposed method that has access to private data. In JavaScript, any exposed method defined within the closure scope is privileged. For example:

```
var o = function o () {
  var data = 1,
    get;

  get = function get() {
    return data;
  };

  return {
    get: get
  };
};

test('Closure for object privacy.', function () {
  var obj = o(); // Get an object with the .get() method.
```

```
    try {
      ok(data, 'This throws an error.');
    } catch (e) {
      ok(true,'The data var is only available'
        + ' to privileged methods.');
    }

    equal(
      obj.get(), 1,
      '.get() should have access to the closure.'
    );
  });
```

In this example, o is an object factory that defines the private variable data and a privileged method, .get(), that has access to it. The factory exposes .get() in the object literal that it returns.

In the test, the return value from o is assigned to the obj variable. In the try block, the attempt to access the private data var throws an error because it is undeclared outside the closure scope.

In addition to the data privacy benefits, closures are an essential ingredient in languages that support first-class functions, because they give you access to outer scope variables from inside your lambdas.

Closures are commonly used to feed data to event handlers or callbacks, which might get triggered long after the containing function has finished. For example:

```
(function () {
  var arr = [],
    count = 1,
    delay = 20,
    timer,
    complete;

  timer = function timer() {
    setTimeout(function inner() {
      arr.push(count);

      if (count < 3) {
        count += 1;
        timer();
      } else {
        complete();
      }
    }, delay);
  };

  asyncTest('Closure with setTimeout.', function () {
    complete = function complete() {
      equal(
        arr.join(','), '1,2,3',
```

```
        'arr should be [1,2,3]'
      );
      start();
    };

    timer();

    equal(
      arr.length, 0,
      'array should be empty until the first timout.'
    );
  });
}());
```

In this example, the `inner()` lambda has access to `arr`, `complete()`, and `count` from the containing function. Its job is to add the current `count` to the array each time it's called. If the array isn't full yet, it calls the `timer()` function to set a new timeout so it will be invoked again after the delay has expired.

This is an example of asynchronous recursion, and the pattern is sometimes used to retry Ajax requests when they fail. There is usually a retry limit and a delay so that the server doesn't get hammered with endless retries from millions of users.

The `asyncTest()` function is provided by QUnit as a shortcut for running asynchronous tests. Normally, you need to call `stop()` at the top of your test to tell QUnit that you're expecting assertions to fire asynchronously. The `stop()` function suspends the completion of the test until `start()` gets called.

When the test runs, the `complete()` function gets defined. It will later be called from `inner()` after all of the timeouts have expired. The complete function defines an `equal()` assertion to verify the contents of `arr`.

As you can see, the final `equal()` assertion in the program listing is actually the first one that gets run. That's because the first timeout has not had time to expire before the JavaScript engine gets to that line in the code. At that point, any attempt to read `arr` or `count` will return the initial values. The values don't get modified until the first timeout expires and `inner()` has had a chance to run.

Each time `inner()` gets called, `count` is incremented and pushed onto the array, `arr`. Since `count` and `arr` were defined inside the closure, it's possible to access them from other functions in the same scope, which is why we can test them in the `asyncTest()` call.

Method Design

Several techniques exist in JavaScript to design method APIs. JavaScript supports named parameter lists, function polymorphism, method chaining, and lambda expressions.

You should be familiar with all of these techniques so that you can choose the right tool for the job.

There are some principles to keep in mind when you design your methods. This bears repeating:

- Keep It Simple, Stupid (KISS)
- Do One Thing (DOT), and do it well
- Don't Repeat Yourself (DRY)

Named Parameters

The number of variables you pass into a function is called its *arity*. Generally speaking, function arity should be kept small, but sometimes you need a wide range of parameters (for example, to initialize the configuration of a module or create a new object instance). The trouble with a large arity is that each parameter must be passed into the function in the right order, even if several parameters are not needed. It can be difficult to remember what order is required, and it doesn't make sense to require a parameter that isn't really required for the function to do its job properly.

This example is designed to set up a new user account. Each user account has some default settings that get honored unless an override value is passed in:

```
var userProto = {
    name: '',
    email: '',
    alias: '',
    showInSearch: true,
    colorScheme: 'light'
};

function createUser(name, email, alias, showInSearch,
  colorScheme) {

  return {
    name: name || userProto.name,
    name: email || userProto.email,
    alias: alias || userProto.alias,
    showInSearch: showInSearch,
    colorScheme: colorScheme || userProto.colorScheme
  };
}

test('User account creation', function () {
  var newUser = createUser('Tonya', '', '', '', 'dark');

  equal(newUser.colorScheme, 'dark',
```

```
                'colorScheme stored correctly.');
    });
```

In this case, the createUser() function takes five optional parameters. The userPro
to object is a prototype (not to be confused with the prototype property). The trouble
with this implementation becomes obvious when you look at the usage in isolation:

```
    var newUser = createUser('Tonya', '', '', '', 'dark');
```

What jumps out immediately is that it's impossible to know what the second, third, or
fourth parameter is without looking at the createUser() implementation. It's also impossible to set the last parameter without passing in values for *all parameters*. What's
more, if you want to add more parameters later or change the order of the parameters,
it's going to be difficult if the function is used frequently.

Here is a better alternative:

```
    var newUser = createUser({
        name: 'Mike',
        showInSearch: false
    });
```

You can implement this easily using the extend method that comes with most popular
libraries (including jQuery and Underscore). Here's how it's done with jQuery:

```
    function createUser(options) {
        return $.extend({}, userProto, options);
    }
```

$.extend() takes objects as its parameters. The first is the object to be extended. In this
case, we want to return a new object so that we don't alter the userProto or options
objects. The other objects (as many as you like) hold the properties and methods you
wish to extend the first object with. This is a simple, elegant way to reuse code.

Function Polymorphism

In computer science, *polymorphism* means that something behaves differently based on
context, like words that have different meanings based on how they're used:

- "Watch out for that sharp turn in the road!"
- "That knife is sharp!"
- "John Resig is sharp! Making the jQuery function polymorphic was a stroke of
  genius."

Polymorphic functions behave differently based on the parameters you pass into them.
In JavaScript, those parameters are stored in the array-like arguments object, but it's
missing useful array methods.

`Array.prototype.slice()` is an easy way to shallow copy some or all of an array (or an array-like object).

You can borrow the `.slice()` method from the `Array` prototype using a technique called *method delegation*. You delegate the `.slice()` call to the `Array.prototype` object. The method call looks like this:

```
var args = Array.prototype.slice.call(arguments, 0);
```

Slice starts at index 0 and returns everything from that index on as a new array. That syntax is a little long winded, though. It's easier and faster to write:

```
var args = [].slice.call(arguments, 0);
```

The square bracket notation creates a new empty array to delegate the slice call to. That sounds like it might be slow, but creating an empty array is actually a very fast operation. I ran an A/B performance test with millions of operations and didn't see a blip in the memory use or any statistically significant difference in operation speed.

You could use this technique to create a function that sorts parameters:

```
function sort() {
  var args = [].slice.call(arguments, 0);
  return args.sort();
}

test('Sort', function () {
  var result = sort('b', 'a', 'c');
  ok(result, ['a', 'b', 'c'], 'Sort works!');
});
```

Because `arguments` is not a real array, it doesn't have the `.sort()` method. However, since a real array is returned from the `.slice()` call, you have access to all of the array methods on the `args` array. The `.sort()` method returns a sorted version of the array.

Polymorphic functions frequently need to examine the first argument in order to decide how to respond. Now that `args` is a real array, you can use the `.shift()` method to get the first argument:

```
var first = args.shift();
```

Now you can branch if a string is passed as the first parameter:

```
function morph(options) {
  var args = [].slice.call(arguments, 0),
    animals = 'turtles'; // Set a default

  if (typeof options === 'string') {
    animals = options;
    args.shift();
  }

  return('The pet store has ' + args + ' ' + animals
```

```
    + '.');
  }

  test('Polymorphic branching.', function () {
    var test1 = morph('cats', 3),
      test2 = morph('dogs', 4),
      test3 = morph(2);

    equal(test1, 'The pet store has 3 cats.', '3 Cats.');
    equal(test2, 'The pet store has 4 dogs.', '4 Dogs.');
    equal(test3, 'The pet store has 2 turtles.',
      'The pet store has 2 turtles.');
  });
```

Method dispatch

Method dispatch is the mechanism that determines what to do when an object receives a message. JavaScript does this by checking to see if the method exists on the object. If it doesn't, the JavaScript engine checks the prototype object. If the method isn't there, it checks the prototype's prototype, and so on. When it finds a matching method, it calls the method and passes the parameters in. This is also known as *behavior delegation* in delegation-based prototypal languages like JavaScript.

Dynamic dispatch enables polymorphism by selecting the appropriate method to run based on the parameters that get passed into the method at runtime. Some languages have special syntax to support dynamic dispatch. In JavaScript, you can check the parameters from within the called method and call another method in response:

```
var methods = {
    init: function (args) {
      return 'initializing...';
    },
    hello: function (args) {
      return 'Hello, ' + args;
    },
    goodbye: function (args) {
      return 'Goodbye, cruel ' + args;
    }
  },
  greet = function greet(options) {
    var args = [].slice.call(arguments, 0),
      initialized = false,
      action = 'init'; // init will run by default

    if (typeof options === 'string' &&
        typeof methods[options] === 'function') {

      action = options;
      args.shift();
    }
```

```
      return methods[action](args);
   };

   test('Dynamic dispatch', function () {
     var test1 = greet(),
       test2 = greet('hello', 'world!'),
       test3 = greet('goodbye', 'world!');

     equal(test2, 'Hello, world!',
       'Dispatched to hello method.');

     equal(test3, 'Goodbye, cruel world!',
       'Dispatched to goodbye method.');
   });
```

This manual style of dynamic dispatch is a common technique in jQuery plug-ins in order to enable developers to add many methods to a plug-in without adding them all to the jQuery prototype (jQuery.fn). Using this technique, you can claim a single name on the jQuery prototype and add as many methods as you like to it. Users then select the method they want to invoke using:

```
$(selection).yourPlugin('methodName', params);
```

Generics and Collection Polymorphism

Generic programming is a style that attempts to express algorithms and data structures in a way that is type agnostic. The idea is that most algorithms can be employed across a variety of different types. Generic programming typically starts with one or more type-specific implementations, which then get *lifted* (abstracted) to create a more generic version that will work with a new set of types.

Generics do not require conditional logic branching to implement an algorithm differently based on the type of data passed in. Rather, the datatypes passed in must support the required features that the algorithm needs in order to work. Those features are called *requirements*, which in turn get collected into sets called *concepts*.

Generics employ *parametric polymorphism*, which uses a single branch of logic applied to generic type parameters. In contrast, *ad-hoc polymorphism* relies on conditional branching to handle the treatment of different parameter types (either built into the language with features like dynamic dispatch or introduced at program design time).

Generic programming is particularly relevant to functional programming because functional programming works best when a simple function vocabulary can express a wide range of functionality, regardless of type.

In most languages, generic programming is concerned with making algorithms work for different types of lists. In JavaScript, any collection (array or object) can contain any type (or mix of types), and most programmers rely on duck typing to accomplish similar goals. (If it walks like a duck and quacks like a duck, treat it like a duck. In other words, if an object has the features you need, assume it's the right kind of object and use it.) Many of the built-in object methods are generics, meaning that they can operate on multiple types of objects.

JavaScript supports two types of collections: objects and arrays. The principle difference between an object and an array is that one is keyed with names and the other sequentially with numbers. Objects don't guarantee any particular order; arrays do. Other than that, both behave pretty much the same. It often makes sense to implement functions that work regardless of which type of collection gets passed in.

Many of the functions you might apply to an array would also work for an object and vice versa. For example, say you want to select a random member from an object or array.

The easiest way to select a random element is to use a numbered index, so if the collection is an object, it could be converted to an array using ad-hoc polymorphism. The following function will do that:

```javascript
var toArray = function toArray(obj) {
  var arr = [],
    prop;

  for (prop in obj) {
    if (obj.hasOwnProperty(prop)) {
      arr.push(prop);
    }
  }
  return arr;
};
```

The `randomItem()` function is easy now. First, you test the type of collection that gets passed in and convert it to an array if it's not one already, and then return a random item from the array using the built-in `Math.random()` method:

```javascript
var randomItem = function randomItem(collection) {
  var arr = ({}.toString.call(collection) !==
    '[object Array]')
      ? toArray(collection)
      : collection;
  return arr[Math.floor(arr.length * Math.random())];
};

test('randomItem()', function () {
  var obj = {
      a: 'a',
      b: 'b',
      c: 'c'
    },
    arr = ['a', 'b', 'c'];

  ok(obj.hasOwnProperty(randomItem(obj)),
```

```
    'randomItem works on Objects.');

  ok(obj.hasOwnProperty(randomItem(arr)),
    'randomItem works on Arrays.');
});
```

These tests check to see if the returned value exists in the test object.

Unlike true generics, this code relies on conditional branching internally to handle objects as a special case. Since arrays are already objects in JavaScript, a lot of what you might do with an object will work for arrays without any conversion. In other words, a lot of functions designed to act on JavaScript objects are truly generic in that they will also work for arrays without any specialized logic (assuming that the array has all of the required features).

Collection polymorphism is a very useful tool for code reuse and API consistency. Many library methods in both jQuery and Underscore work on both objects and arrays.

JavaScript 1.6 introduced a number of new built-in array and string generics. With 1.6 compatible JavaScript engines, you can use array methods such as .every() on strings:

```
var validString = 'abc',
  invalidString = 'abcd',

  validArray = ['a', 'b', 'c'],
  invalidArray = ['a', 'b', 'c', 'd'],

  isValid = function isValid(char) {
    return validString.indexOf(char) >= 0;
  };

test('Array String generics', function () {
  ok(![].every.call(invalidString, isValid),
    'invalidString is rejected.');

  ok([].every.call(validString, isValid),
    'validString passes.');

  ok(![].every.call(invalidArray, isValid),
    'invalidArray is rejected.');

  ok([].every.call(validArray, isValid),
    'validArray passes.');
});
```

You can also use string methods on numbers:

```
var num = 303;

test('String number generics', function () {
  var i = ''.indexOf.call(num, 0);
```

```
  ok(i === 1,
    'String methods work on numbers.');
});
```

Method Chaining and Fluent APIs

Method chaining is using the output of one method call as the context of the next method call. For example, in jQuery you often see things like:

```
$('.friend').hide().filter('.active').show();
```

Perhaps better:

```
$('.friend')
  .hide()
  .filter('.active')
  .show();
```

This translates to: "find all elements with the `friend` class and hide them, then find the friends with the `active` class and show them."

On page load, our friends list looks like this:

```
* Mick
* Hunz (active)
* Yannis
```

After running the code above, it looks like this:

```
* Hunz (active)
```

One of the primary benefits of method chaining is that it can be used to support fluent APIs. In short, a *fluent API* is one that reads like natural language. That doesn't mean that it has to look like English, but fluent APIs often use real verbs as method calls (like hide and show).

jQuery is a great example of a fluent API. In fact, jQuery's fluency makes it one of the easiest libraries to learn and use. Almost everything that jQuery does was already available in other libraries when jQuery was first released. What made jQuery stand out was the easy-to-learn vocabulary. Almost every jQuery statement reads something like this: "Find all the elements matching a selector, then do x, then y, then z. Selection, verb, verb..."

Chaining has its disadvantages. It can encourage you to do too much in a single line of code, it can encourage you to write too much procedural code, and it can be difficult to debug. It's tough to set a breakpoint in the middle of a chain.

If you get into a tight spot debugging a chain, remember you can always capture the output at any step in the chain with a variable assignment and resume the chain by calling the next method on that variable. In fact, you don't have to chain at all to use a fluent API.

There's more to fluency than chaining. The salient point is that fluent methods are made to work together to express functionality in the same way that words in a language work together to express ideas. That means that they output objects with methods that make sense to call on the resulting data.

Building a fluent API is a lot like building a miniature domain-specific language (DSL). We'll go into detail about how to build a fluent API in Chapter 3.

It's easy to go too far with fluent APIs. In other languages, fluent APIs are frequently used to configure a new object. Since JavaScript supports object-literal notation, this is almost certainly a bad use of fluency in JavaScript.

Fluency can also lead to unnecessary verbosity. For example, the Should.js API encourages you to write long sentences with strung-together dot notation access. Keep it simple.

Functional Programming

Functional programming is a style of programming that uses *higher-order functions* (as opposed to objects and data) to facilitate code organization and reuse. A higher order function treats functions as data, either taking a function as an argument or returning a function as a result. Higher order functions are very powerful code reuse tools that are commonly used in JavaScript for a variety of purposes. Here are a few examples:

They can be used to *abstract algorithms from datatypes.* This is important because it reduces the amount of code you need in order to support various datatypes in your reusable algorithms. Without this, you might create a special function to operate on a collection of one type, and a similar, but slightly different function to operate on another. This is a very common problem in most applications.

A series of functions that do essentially the same thing and differ only in the type of data they operate on is a serious code smell. You're violating the DRY principle, one of the most valuable guidelines available to you in software design.

For example, imagine you have to sort two lists of items by price, but one is a list of concerts where the price is called `ticketPrice`, and another is a list of books where the price is just `price`.

Of course, you could attempt to squeeze both into a single, more generic type and create a generic function that will work with both (using duck typing), but that might require an unjustifiable refactor.

Instead, you could pass in a function to handle the comparison for the sort:

```
var shows = [
    {
      artist: 'Kreap',
      city: 'Melbourne',
      ticketPrice: '40'
    },
    {
      artist: 'DJ EQ',
      city: 'Paris',
      ticketPrice: '38'
    },
    {
      artist: 'Treasure Fingers',
      city: 'London',
      ticketPrice: '60'
    }
  ],
  books = [
    {
      title: 'How to DJ Proper',
      price: '18'
    },
    {
      title: 'Music Marketing for Dummies',
      price: '26'
    },
    {
      title: 'Turntablism for Beginners',
      price: '15'
    }
  ];

test('Datatype abstraction', function () {
  var sortedShows = shows.sort(function (a, b) {
      return a.ticketPrice < b.ticketPrice;
    }),
    sortedBooks = books.sort(function (a, b) {
      return a.price < b.price;
    });
  ok(sortedShows[0].ticketPrice >
    sortedShows[2].ticketPrice,
    'Shows sorted correctly.');
  ok(sortedBooks[0].price >
    sortedBooks[1].price,
    'Books sorted correctly.');
});
```

Higher-order functions are very commonly used to *abstract list iteration boilerplate from algorithm implementation.* You may have noticed in the previous example that the built-in `Array.prototype.sort()` method handles the iteration details internally, so you don't even have to think about writing a for loop. You frequently see a pattern like this repeated in most code:

```
test('Traditional for loop', function () {
  var i,
    length = books.length;

  for (i = 0; i < length; i++) {
    books[i].category = 'music';
  }

  ok(books[0].category === 'music',
    'Books have categories.');
});
```

There are several functional methods available whose sole purpose is to iterate through a collection in order to process it with a passed in function of your choice. The most basic of the array iterators is .forEach(). For example, imagine you want to add a category field to each of the book items. Using .forEach(), you don't have to worry about writing the loop or keeping track of the iteration index. You simply write the function that you'll use to process the list:

```
test('Iterator abstraction', function () {
  books.forEach(function (book) {
    book.category = 'music';
  });

  ok(books[0].category === 'music',
    'Books have categories.');
});
```

Another common use of higher order functions is to support *partial application and currying* (see "Partial Application and Currying" on page 40).

Stateless Functions (aka Pure Functions)

Pure functions are stateless. This means that they do not use or modify variables, objects, or arrays that were defined outside the function. Given the same inputs, stateless functions will always return the same output. Stateless functions won't break if you call them at different times.

Here's an example of a function that is not pure:

```
var rotate = function rotate(arr) {
  arr.push(arr.shift());
  return arr;
}

test('Rotate', function () {
  var original = [1, 2, 3];
```

```
    deepEqual(rotate(original), [2,3,1],
      'rotate() should rotate array elements.');

    // Fails! Original array gets mutated.
    deepEqual(original, [1,2,3],
      'Should not mutate external data.');
});
```

Pure functions won't mutate external data:

```
var safeRotate = function safeRotate(arr) {
  var newArray = arr.slice(0);
  newArray.push(newArray.shift());
  return newArray;
}

test('safeRotate', function () {
  var original = [1, 2, 3];

  deepEqual(safeRotate(original), [2,3,1],
    'safeRotate() should rotate array elements.');

  // Passes.
  deepEqual(original, [1,2,3],
    'Should not mutate external data.');
});
```

That feature is particularly useful in JavaScript applications, because you often need to manage a lot of asynchronous events. Consequently, time becomes a major factor in code organization.

Because you don't have to worry about clobbering shared data, stateless functions can often be run in parallel, meaning that it's much easier to scale computation horizontally across a large number of worker nodes. In other words, stateless functions are great for high-concurrency applications.

Stateless functions can be chained together for stream processing (i.e., enumerator, processor, [processor], [processor], ..., collector).

Stateless functions can be abstracted and shared as context-agnostic modules.

 To maximize code reuse, try to make as many functions as possible both stateless and generic (or polymorphic). Many jQuery methods satisfy both requirements. Such functions tend to be very useful library methods.

Partial Application and Currying

Partial application wraps a function that takes multiple arguments and returns a function that takes fewer arguments. It uses closures to *fix* one or more arguments so that you only need to supply the arguments that are unknown. Imagine you have a function multiply(), which takes two arguments, x and y, and you notice that you often call the function to multiply by specific numbers. You could create a generic function that will fix one parameter:

```
var multiply = function multiply(x, y) {
    return x * y;
},

partial = function partial(fn) {
    // Drop the function from the arguments list and
    // fix arguments in the closure.
    var args = [].slice.call(arguments, 1);

    // Return a new function with fixed arguments.
    return function() {
        // Combine fixed arguments with new arguments
        // and call fn with them.
        var combinedArgs = args.concat(
            [].slice.call(arguments));
        return fn.apply(this, combinedArgs);
    };
},

double = partial(multiply, 2);

test('Partial application', function () {
    equal(double(4), 8,
        'partial() works.');
});
```

As of ES5, you can also use Function.prototype.bind() for partial application. The only disadvantage is that you won't be able to override the value of this with .call() or .apply(). If your function uses this, you shouldn't use .bind(). This is how you use .bind() for partial application, using the same multiply function:

```
var boundDouble = multiply.bind(null, 2); // null context

test('Partial application with bind', function () {
    equal(boundDouble(4), 8,
        '.bind() should allow partial application.');
});
```

You may have heard this process described as *currying*. The two are commonly confused, but there is a difference. Currying is the process of transforming a function that takes multiple arguments into a chain of functions, each of which takes no more than one argument.

An add function add(1, 2, 3) would become add(1)(2)(3) in curried form, where the first call returns a function that returns another function, and so on. This concept is important in lambda calculus (the inspiration for the lisp family of languages, from which JavaScript borrows heavily). However, since JavaScript supports multiple arguments, it's not common to see true currying in JavaScript applications.

Asynchronous Operations

Asynchronous operations are operations that happen outside the linear flow of program execution. Normally, the JavaScript engine will execute code line by line, in order from top to bottom, following the normal flow of your program (such as function calls, conditional logic, etc.).

Asynchronous operations are broken up into two phases: call and response. By definition, it's impossible to know at what point in the program flow you'll be when you receive an asynchronous response. There are a couple of popular ways to manage that uncertainty.

Callbacks

Callbacks are functions that you pass as arguments to be invoked when the callee has finished its job. Callbacks are commonly passed into event handlers, Ajax requests, and timers. You should already be familiar with passing callbacks to event listeners and timers:

```
var $button = $('<button class="select">Click</button>')
  .appendTo('body');


asyncTest('Async callback event listener.', function () {
  $button.on('click', function clicked() {
    ok(true, 'Button clicked.');
    start();
  });

  setTimeout(function timedOut() {
    $button.click();
    $button.remove();
  }, 20);
});
```

In this code, the clicked() callback gets passed into into jQuery's .on() method. When $button receives a click event, it invokes clicked(), which runs the ok() assertion and then start(), which tells QUnit that it's finished waiting for asynchronous operations so it can continue to run tests.

Next, the timedOut() callback is passed into setTimeout(), which triggers the click event on $button and removes the button from the DOM.

Callbacks work great when you're only waiting for one operation at a time, or when you only have one job to do when the response comes back, but what if you need to manage multiple asynchronous dependencies or you have several unrelated tasks waiting on the same data (such as a provider authorization)? That's where promises can be very useful.

Promises and Deferreds

Promises are objects that allow you to add callback functions to success or failure queues. Instead of calling a callback function in response to the completion of an asynchronous (or synchronous) operation, you return a promise, which allows you to register any number of callbacks.

The promise provides access to the state of the operation: whether it's waiting or finished, and in some cases, what the progress is. You can add callbacks to a promise at any time, which will trigger after the operation is complete and the promise is resolved. If the promise has already resolved, the callback will be invoked immediately.

Promises were popularized in JavaScript by jQuery, inspired by the CommonJS Promises/A design. jQuery uses them internally to manage asynchronous operations, such as Ajax. In fact, as of jQuery 1.5, all jQuery Ajax methods return a promise. Here's how they work:

```
var whenDataFetched = $.getJSON(
  'https://graph.facebook.com/jsapplications'
);

asyncTest('Ajax promise API', function () {
  whenDataFetched
    .done(function (response) {
      ok(response,
        'The server returned data.');
      start();
    })
    .fail(function () {
      ok(true,
        'There was an error.');
      start();
    });
});
```

This example demonstrates an Ajax request to get the page metadata for the "Programming JavaScript Applications" page. Since all of jQuery's Ajax helper functions return a promise, you can add a success callback with `whenDataFetched.done()`.

The difference between a promise and a callback is that a promise is an object that gets returned from the callee, instead of a function that gets passed into and invoked by the callee. With promises, it's much easier to add additional callbacks if you need them and to isolate those callbacks from each other so that the callback code can be organized independently of the initiating call.

A *deferred* is the object that controls the promise, with a few extra methods. jQuery's `.Deferred()` returns a new object that does everything a promise does but also provides `.resolve()` and `.reject()` methods that trigger the corresponding callbacks. For example, say you want to make `setTimeout()` a little more flexible so that you can add callbacks to it at any time and break the need to attach a callback at the timer start time. You could implement it like this:

```
var timer = function timer(delay) {
  var whenTimedOut = $.Deferred(),
    promise = whenTimedOut.promise();

  promise.cancel = function (payload) {
    whenTimedOut.reject(payload);
  };

  setTimeout(function () {
    whenTimedOut.resolve();
  }, delay);

  return promise;
};
asyncTest('Deferred', function () {
  var startTime = new Date(),
    delay = 30,
    afterTimeout = 50,
    cancelTime = 100,
    myTimer = timer(delay),
    cancelTimer = timer(cancelTime);

  expect(4);

  myTimer.done(function () {
    ok(true,
      'First callback fired.');
  });

  myTimer.done(function () {
    var now = new Date();
    ok((now - startTime) > delay,
      'Delay works.'
      );
  });

  setTimeout(function () {
    ok(true,
      'Fires after timeout expires.');
  }, afterTimeout);
```

```
setTimeout(function () {
  start();
}, afterTimeout + 20);

cancelTimer
  .done(function () {
    ok(false,
      'A canceled timer should NOT run .done().');
  })
  .fail(function () {
    ok(true,
      'A canceled timer calls .fail().');
  })
  .cancel();
});
```

Promises really shine when you need to orchestrate a complex sequence of events. It's sometimes necessary to gather data from multiple sources prior to getting data from yet another source.

With callbacks, that can be complicated. With promises, it's easy to wait for any number of promises to resolve before moving on to the next step. Using the `timer()` function as previously defined:

```
var a = timer(60),
  b = timer(70),
  c = timer(40),
  tasks = [a, b, c];

asyncTest('Multiple dependencies.', function () {
  $.when(a, b, c).done(function () {
    ok(true, 'Runs when all promises resolve');
    start();
  });
});
```

Conclusion

I hope by now you're starting to see functions in a whole new light. I could write an entire book about the things you can do with functions when you have the ability to create lambda expressions and closures. For more on functional programming in Java-Script, you may want to read "JavaScript Allongé: A Strong Cup of Functions, Objects, Combinators, and Decorators," by Reginald Braithwaite (*https://leanpub.com/javascript-allonge*).

Functions in JavaScript are so powerful, in fact, that they can completely replace the need for objects. A closure can actually act like an object, and a full-fledged object system can be built using closures. In other words, with all of the functional capabilities built into JavaScript, it doesn't need objects at all to be a great language. But it has them anyway. This reminds me of a story from the MIT Lightweight Languages discussion list (*http://people.csail.mit.edu/gregs/ll1-discuss-archive-html/msg03277.html*), by Anton van Straaten:

> The venerable master Qc Na was walking with his student, Anton. Hoping to prompt the master into a discussion, Anton said "Master, I have heard that objects are a very good thing—is this true?" Qc Na looked pityingly at his student and replied, "Foolish pupil—objects are merely a poor man's closures."

> Chastised, Anton took his leave from his master and returned to his cell, intent on studying closures. He carefully read the entire "Lambda: The Ultimate..." series of papers and its cousins, and implemented a small Scheme interpreter with a closure-based object system. He learned much, and looked forward to informing his master of his progress.

> On his next walk with Qc Na, Anton attempted to impress his master by saying "Master, I have diligently studied the matter, and now understand that objects are truly a poor man's closures." Qc Na responded by hitting Anton with his stick, saying "When will you learn? Closures are a poor man's object." At that moment, Anton became enlightened.

## CHAPTER 3

Objects

With the combination of prototypal inheritance, dynamic object extension, and closures, JavaScript has one of the most flexible and expressive object systems available in any popular programing language.

In JavaScript, all types of functions, arrays, key/value pairs, and data structures in general are really objects. Even primitive types get the object treatment when you refer to them with the property access notations. They get automatically wrapped with an object so that you can call their prototype methods. For example:

```
'tonya@example.com'.split('@')[1]; // => example.com
```

 Primitive types behave like objects when you use the property access notations, but you can't assign new properties to them. Primitives get wrapped with an object temporarily, and then that object is immediately thrown away. Any attempt to assign values to properties will seem to succeed, but subsequent attempts to access that new property will fail.

JavaScript's object system is so powerful and expressive that most of the complexity in common OO patterns melts away when you reproduce them in JavaScript. You simply don't need all of the common cruft to accomplish the stated goals. For instance, because JavaScript is classless, and it's possible to create an object on demand at the precise moment it's needed (lazy instantiation), the singleton is reduced to an object literal:

```
var highlander = {
    name: 'McLeod',
    catchphrase: 'There can be only one.'
};
```

As you continue through this chapter, you'll see that much of the overhead associated with several other GoF design patterns (*http://bit.ly/1pwzcUc*) melts away when you understand how to take advantage of JavaScript's native object capabilities.

You may be aware that JavaScript is not a classical OO language. It's a prototypal language. However, most JavaScript training materials ignore some of the implications of that paradigm shift. It's time to get a firmer handle on exactly what *prototypal* means and how you can take advantage of it to write better, faster, more readable, and more efficient code. It might help to get a better sense of the shortcomings of classical inheritance first.

Classical Inheritance Is Obsolete

> Those who are unaware they are walking in darkness will never seek the light.
>
> —Bruce Lee

In *Design Patterns: Elements of Reusable Object Oriented Software*, the Gang of Four opened the book with two foundational principles of object-oriented design:

1. Program to an interface, not an implementation.
2. *Favor object composition over class inheritance.*

In a sense, the second principle could follow from the first, because inheritance exposes the parent class to all child classes. The child classes are all programming to an implementation, not an interface. Classical inheritance breaks the principle of encapsulation and tightly couples the child class to its ancestors.

Think of it this way: *classical inheritance is like Ikea furniture.* You have a bunch of pieces that are designed to fit together in a very specific way. If everything goes exactly according to plan, chances are high that you'll come out with a usable piece of furniture; but if anything at all goes wrong or deviates from the preplanned specification, there is little room for adjustment or flexibility. Here's where the analogy (and the furniture and the software) breaks down: the design is in a constant state of change.

Composition is more like Lego blocks. The various pieces aren't designed to fit with any specific piece. Instead, they are all designed to fit together with any other piece, with few exceptions.

When you design for classical inheritance, you design a child class to inherit from a specific parent class. The specific parent class name is usually hardcoded right in the child class, with no mechanism to override it. Right from the start, you're boxing yourself in—limiting the ways that you can reuse your code without rethinking its design at a fundamental level.

When you design for composition, the sky is the limit. As long as you can successfully avoid colliding with properties from other source objects, objects can be composed and reused virtually any way you see fit. Once you get the hang of it, composition affords a tremendous amount of freedom compared to classical inheritance. For people who have been immersed in classical inheritance for years and learn how to take real advantage of composition (specifically using prototypal techniques), it is like walking out of a dark tunnel into the light and seeing a whole new world of possibilities open up for you.

Back to *Design Patterns*. Why is the seminal work on object-oriented design so distinctly anti-inheritance? Because inheritance causes several problems:

Tight coupling
> Inheritance is the tightest coupling available in OO design. Descendant classes have an intimate knowledge of their ancestor classes.

Inflexible hierarchies
> Single-parent hierarchies are rarely capable of describing all possible use cases. Eventually, all hierarchies are "wrong" for new uses—a problem that necessitates code duplication.

Multiple inheritance is complicated
> It's often desirable to inherit from more than one parent. That process is inordinately complex, and its implementation is inconsistent with the process for single inheritance, which makes it harder to read and understand.

Brittle architecture
> With tight coupling, it's often difficult to refactor a class with the "wrong" design, because much existing functionality depends on the existing design.

The gorilla/banana problem
> There are often parts of the parent that you don't want to inherit. Subclassing allows you to override properties from the parent, but it doesn't allow you to select which properties you want to inherit.

These problems are summed up nicely by Joe Armstrong in *Coders at Work* by Peter Siebel (*http://www.codersatwork.com/*):

> The problem with object-oriented languages is they've got all this implicit environment that they carry around with them. You wanted a banana but what you got was a gorilla holding the banana and the entire jungle.

Inheritance works beautifully for a short time, but eventually the app architecture becomes arthritic. When you've built up your entire app on a foundation of classical inheritance, the dependencies on ancestors run so deep that even reusing or changing trivial amounts of code can turn into a gigantic refactor. Deep inheritance trees are brittle, inflexible, and difficult to extend.

More often than not, what you wind up with in a mature classical OO application is a range of possible ancestors to inherit from, all with slightly different but often similar configurations. Figuring out which to use is not straightforward, and you soon have a haphazard collection of similar objects with unexpectedly divergent properties. Around this time, people start throwing around the word "rewrite" as if it's an easier undertaking than refactoring the current mess.

Many of the patterns in the GoF book were designed specifically to address these well-known problems. In many ways, the book itself can be read as a critique of the short-comings of most classical OO languages, along with the accompanying lengthy work-arounds. In short, patterns point out deficiencies in the language. You can reproduce all of the GoF patterns in JavaScript, but before you start using them as blueprints for your JavaScript code, you'll want to get a good handle on JavaScript's prototypal and functional capabilities.

For a long time, many people were confused about whether JavaScript is truly object-oriented, because they felt it lacked features from other OO languages. Setting aside the fact that JavaScript handles classical inheritance with less code than most class-based languages, coming to JavaScript and asking how to do classical inheritance is like picking up a touch-screen mobile phone and asking where the rotary dial is. Of course, people will be amused when the next thing out of your mouth is, "If it doesn't have a rotary dial, it's not a telephone!"

JavaScript can do most of the OO things you're accustomed to in other languages, such as inheritance, data privacy, and polymorphism. However, JavaScript has many native capabilities that make some classical OO features and patterns obsolete. It's better to stop asking, "How do I do classical inheritance in JavaScript?" and start asking, "What cool new things does JavaScript enable me to do?"

 I wish I could tell you that you'll never have to deal with classical inheritance in JavaScript. Unfortunately, because classical inheritance is easy to mimic in JavaScript, and many people come from class-based programming backgrounds, there are several popular libraries that feature classical inheritance prominently, including Backbone.js, which you'll have a chance to explore soon. When you do encounter situations in which you're forced to subclass by other programmers, keep in mind that inheritance hierarchies should be kept as small as possible. Avoid subclassing subclasses, remember that you can mix and match different code reuse styles, and things will go more smoothly.

Fluent-Style JavaScript

> I have not invented a "new style," composite, modified, or otherwise that is set within distinct form as apart from "this" method or "that" method. On the contrary, I hope to free my followers from clinging to styles, patterns, or molds.
>
> ...The extraordinary part of it lies in its simplicity.
>
> —Bruce Lee

Programmers with a background in other languages are like immigrants to JavaScript. They often code with an *accent*—preconceived notions about how to solve problems. For example, programmers with a background in classical OO tend to have a hard time letting constructors go. Using constructor functions is a clear and strong accent, because they are completely unnecessary in JavaScript. They are a waste of time and energy.

Unfortunately, most JavaScript learning materials will teach you that you build objects using constructor functions.

There are serious limitations to this way of doing things. The first is that you must always call a constructor using the new keyword. Failing to do so will pass the global object in as this. Your properties and methods will clobber the global namespace. If you instantiate more than one object, they will not be instance safe. In strict mode, the situation when you forget new is a little different: this is useless, and trying to assign properties to it will throw an error.

There's a simple workaround that requires a boilerplate check inside every constructor function, but since any function can return an object in JavaScript, you end up using new sometimes, but not all the time. A convention has sprung up in JavaScript to help you remember when to use new and when not to. Constructor functions always begin with a capital letter. If you're calling a function that begins with a capital letter, use new. Unfortunately, lots of library developers uppercase the first letter of their library namespace, regardless of whether or not it's a constructor function, so even that solution is less than ideal. And that's not even the real problem.

The real problem is that using constructors will almost always get you stuck thinking in classical OO mode. The constructor becomes analogous to a class. You might start to think, "I want to subclass x..." and that's where you get into trouble. You're ignoring two of the best features of JavaScript: dynamic object extension (you can add properties to any object in JavaScript after instantiation) and prototypal inheritance. The two combined are a much more powerful and flexible way to reuse code than classical inheritance.

Programmers who learned JavaScript as a first language are far less likely to be attached to classical OO and inheritance, because it's harder to implement in JavaScript than the simpler, *native* alternatives. You can learn a lot about JavaScript by reading the code of experienced JavaScript natives who have not been influenced by classical inheritance.

Most languages have many different accents and grammars. In fact, almost all disciplines spin off into different schools of thought. Martial arts has kickboxing, jui jitsu, boxing, karate, kung fu, and so on. Each emphasizes different philosophies, mechanics, and core techniques. In his famous book, *The Tao of Jeet Kun Do*, Bruce Lee advised that you develop your own style. Study and take in all the good things about different styles, pick what you like, and discard the rest to create your own unique style. It's good advice that lies at the heart of mixed martial arts—a discipline that combines the best features of several fighting styles.

The same is true with programming languages. JavaScript itself is a fusion of the best ideas from Scheme (lambda), Self (prototypal inheritance), and Java (syntax).

To coin a phrase, *fluent style* simply discards inefficient constructs and takes advantage of JavaScript's strengths and efficiencies:

Lambdas and closures
These are a language unto themselves. Lambda expressions are simple, elegant, and powerful. Literally anything that can be expressed as a computable algorithm can be expressed through lambdas. Lambdas are an essential ingredient of functional programming.

Object-literal notation
This is the fastest route to a working object instance from scratch. Also take advantage of its sibling, *array literal notation*.

Dynamic object extension
This allows you to easily use mixins, composition, and aggregation for code reuse, even after object instantiation. Subclassing requires a lot of extra typing and gains you nothing. It makes your code brittle and inflexible.

Prototypes
These allow you to clone instances of existing objects to create new ones and share generic methods on a delegate object.

Factories
These are a more flexible and less verbose alternative to constructor functions in JavaScript. You don't need constructors to create new objects. Any function in JavaScript can return a new object, and with less code than a constructor requires. Unlike constructors, factories hide instantiation details from the caller, and there's no need to use the awkward and superfluous new keyword when invoking a factory. Factories make it easy to combine any of the above techniques, and even change implementations at runtime without changing the way that objects are instantiated from outside the factory.

Fluent APIs (not to be confused with fluent-style JavaScript)

> A fluent API is an interface that reads a bit like natural language. Fluent APIs are usually chainable but don't need to be chained to be fluent. The defining characteristic is that each method returns an object that has additional methods on it that make sense as a next step. In this way, methods can be strung together in short sentences, each method acting on the return value of the last. jQuery and Jasmine are examples of popular fluent APIs in JavaScript.

Some of the techniques used in fluent-style JavaScript were popularized by the Prototype and jQuery libraries, but fluent style wasn't invented by anybody in particular. There isn't anything new or unique about it that hasn't been said a thousand times before. It's simply the natural evolution of a language with this particular blend of features at its core. It is not a style in itself so much as the shedding of unnecessary styles and techniques that are often habits left over from other languages.

Even giving "fluent style" a name seems a bit silly. It's necessary only to distinguish it from the cumbersome styles taught in most JavaScript books and tutorials. In short, fluent style isn't really a particular formal style—*it's just what fluent JavaScripters do.*

As time marches on, it's natural to assume that fluent-style JavaScript will and should evolve beyond this definition as new efficiencies are discovered and popularized and new features are added to the language.

Prototypes

A *prototype* is an object intended to model other objects after. It is similar to a class in that you can use it to construct any number of object instances, but different in the sense that it is an object itself. There are two ways that prototypes can be used: you can delegate access to a single, shared prototype object (called a delegate), or you can make clones of the prototype.

Delegate Prototypes

In JavaScript, objects have an internal reference to a delegate prototype. When an object is queried for a property or method, the JavaScript engine first checks the object. If the key doesn't exist on that object, it checks the delegate prototype, and so on up the prototype chain. The prototype chain typically ends at the Object prototype.

When you create an object literal, it automatically attaches the Object prototype. Alternatively, you can specify a prototype to set when you create an object via the Object.create() method. Object.create() was added with ES5, so you may need to polyfill it. Here's the Object.create() polyfill from the Mozilla Developer Network documentation (*http://mzl.la/1pFH3jo*):

```
if (!Object.create) {
  Object.create = function (o) {
```

```
        if (arguments.length > 1) {
            throw new Error('Object.create implementation'
            + ' only accepts the first parameter.');
        }
        function F() {}
        F.prototype = o;
        return new F();
    };
}
```

When you invoke a constructor with the new keyword, the object referenced by the constructor's prototype property gets set as the delegate for the newly created object. As you can see, this Object.create() polyfill is simply a shortcut that creates a new constructor function, sets the object you pass in as the constructor's prototype property, and then returns a new object with that prototype. Here's how you use it:

```
var switchProto = {
    isOn: function isOn() {
        return this.state;
    },

    toggle: function toggle() {
        this.state = !this.state;
        return this;
    },

    state: false
    },
    switch1 = Object.create(switchProto),
    switch2 = Object.create(switchProto);

test('Object.create', function () {
    ok(switch1.toggle().isOn(),
        '.toggle() works.'
    );

    ok(!switch2.isOn(),
        'instance safe.'
    );
});
```

Simply pass any object into Object.create(), and it will be be set as the delegate pro-totype for the newly created object. As you can see, the delegate prototype has some special behavior.

Notice that state is on the prototype, but changing state on switch1 did not change state on switch2. Properties on the prototype act like defaults. When you set them on the instance, the instance value overrides the value for that instance, only.

It's important to note though that if you mutate an object or array property on the prototype, that mutation will be shared on the prototype. If you replace the whole property, the change is reflected only on that instance:

```
var switchProto = {
    isOn: function isOn() {
      return this.state;
    },

    toggle: function toggle() {
      this.state = !this.state;
      return this;
    },

    meta: {
      name: 'Light switch'
    },

    state: false
  },
  switch1 = Object.create(switchProto),
  switch2 = Object.create(switchProto);

test('Prototype mutations.', function () {
  switch2.meta.name = 'Breaker switch';

  equal(switch1.meta.name, 'Breaker switch',
    'Object and array mutations are shared.'
  );

  switch2.meta = { name: 'Power switch' };

  equal(switch1.meta.name, 'Breaker switch',
    'Property replacement is instance-specific.'
  );
});
```

In the code, `switchProto` has a property called `meta`. When you change a subproperty of meta, it mutates the object attached to the prototype; but when you replace the whole meta object with a new object, it overrides the property for that instance only.

 Sharing state (nonmethod data) on a prototype property is commonly considered an anti-pattern in the JavaScript community, because accidental mutations of shared properties are a common source of bugs when you do it.

Prototype Cloning

Sometimes you don't want to share data on a prototype property. Instead, you want each instance to have its own unique copy of the prototype's properties. Popular JavaScript libraries have been shipping with a suitable method for cloning prototypes for several years. The cloning method is usually called .extend(). You pass in an object to extend, followed by any number of objects to extend from.

Unfortunately, extend() is not included in the JavaScript specification yet (Object.as sign() works very similarly and is in JavaScript ES6). extend() is included in both jQuery and Underscore, and its implementation is simple. Here is the source from Underscore:

```
_.extend = function(obj) {
  each(slice.call(arguments, 1), function(source) {
    for (var prop in source) {
      obj[prop] = source[prop];
    }
  });
  return obj;
};
```

As you can see, it takes the first argument as a target (obj), iterates through remaining source arguments, and copies all of the public properties from each source to the target obj. The last object you pass in takes precedence if there are any property collisions.

Here's how you use it to clone a prototype object:

```
var switchProto = {
    isOn: function isOn() {
      return this.state;
    },

    toggle: function toggle() {
      this.state = !this.state;
      return this;
    },

    meta: {
      name: 'Light switch'
    },

    state: false
  },

  switch1 = extend({}, switchProto),
  switch2 = extend({}, switchProto);

  test('Prototype clones.', function () {

    switch1.isOn.isShared = true;
```

```
  ok(!switch2.isShared,
    'Methods are copied for each instance, not shared.'
  );

  ok(switch1.toggle().isOn(),
    '.toggle() works.'
  );

  ok(!switch2.isOn(),
    'instance safe.'
  );

  switch2.meta.name = 'Breaker switch';

  equal(switch1.meta.name, 'Breaker switch',
    'Object and array mutations are shared.'
  );

  switch2.meta = { name: 'Power switch' };

  equal(switch1.meta.name, 'Breaker switch',
    'Property replacement is instance-specific.'
  );
});
```

In the `extend()` calls, you pass the new, empty object {} as the destination object, followed by the prototype `switchProto` as the source object.

The primary difference between cloning and delegation is that cloning will copy the value of each property for every object instance, whereas delegation is more memory efficient. It stores only one copy of each default property setting until you need to override properties at the instance level.

As it turns out, it's often a good idea to employ a mix of both techniques—using the delegate prototype to share public methods between objects and cloning for data that can't be safely shared between instances.

The Flyweight Pattern

The *flyweight pattern* conserves system resources by storing all reusable properties and methods on a delegate object, as opposed to storing copies of them on every instance. This can save a lot of memory and improve system performance dramatically if there are many objects of the same type.

In other languages, you have to jump through some hoops to set up a delegate object and defer all method calls and access to it. In JavaScript, the delegate prototype serves as a built-in flyweight delegate. You don't need to worry about wiring it up yourself.

Imagine you're programming a video game and there is a common enemy that has dozens or hundreds of copies in the game world. Each copy stores the enemy's base stats, such as strength and speed, along with methods for all of its attacks and defenses. It also stores the enemy's position in the game world and current health. You can optimize these objects in JavaScript by storing all of that data on the enemy prototype. When there is a change to the enemy's health or position, those changes are made to the enemy instance, while all the other data and methods are delegated to the prototype:

```javascript
var enemyPrototype = {
    name: 'Wolf',
    position: { // Override this with setPosition
      x: 0,
      y: 0
    },
    setPosition: function setPosition (x, y) {
      this.position = {
        x: x,
        y: y
      };
      return this;
    },
    health: 20, // Overrides automatically on change
    bite: function bite() {
    },
    evade: function evade() {
    }
  },

  spawnEnemy = function () {
    return Object.create(enemyPrototype);
  };

test('Flyweight pattern.', function () {
  var wolf1 = spawnEnemy(),
    wolf2 = spawnEnemy();

  wolf1.health = 5;
  ok(wolf2.health = 20,
    'Primitives override automatically.');

  ok(wolf1.setPosition(10, 10)
      .position.x === 10, 'Object override works.');
  equal(wolf2.position.x, 0,
      'The prototype should remain unchanged.');
});
```

Because moving data to the prototype delegate is so easy in JavaScript, it's common to employ the flyweight pattern for nearly all object methods. That's what's going on when you see lines like this:

```
MyConstructor.prototype.myMethod = function () {
  // A method to be shared...
};
```

It's less common to see the prototype employed for member data, but it's a perfectly reasonable place to store default values that are commonly reused. Just be mindful that you'll need to replace member objects and arrays rather than mutate them in place if you want your changes to be instance safe.

Object Creation

Objects in JavaScript are sometimes created with constructor functions. For example:

```
function Car(color, direction, mph) {
  this.color = color || 'pink';
  this.direction = direction || 0; // 0 = Straight ahead
  this.mph = mph || 0;

  this.gas = function gas(amount) {
    amount = amount || 10;
    this.mph += amount;
    return this;
  };

  this.brake = function brake(amount) {
    amount = amount || 10;
    this.mph = ((this.mph - amount) < 0)? 0
      : this.mph - amount;
    return this;
  };
}

var myCar = new Car();

test('Constructor', function () {
  ok(myCar.color, 'Has a color');

  equal(myCar.gas().mph, 10,
    '.accelerate() should add 10mph.'
  );

  equal(myCar.brake(5).mph, 5,
    '.brake(5) should subtract 5mph.'
  );
});
```

You can get data encapsulation by using private variables:

```
function Car(color, direction, mph) {
  var isParkingBrakeOn = false;
  this.color = color || 'pink';
  this.direction = direction || 0; // 0 = Straight ahead
```

```
      this.mph = mph || 0;

      this.gas = function gas(amount) {
        amount = amount || 10;
        this.mph += amount;
        return this;
      };
      this.brake = function brake(amount) {
        amount = amount || 10;
        this.mph = ((this.mph - amount) < 0)? 0
          : this.mph - amount;
        return this;
      };
      this.toggleParkingBrake = function toggleParkingBrake() {
        isParkingBrakeOn = !isParkingBreakOn;
        return this;
      };
      this.isParked = function isParked() {
        return isParkingBrakeOn;
      }
    }

    var myCar = new Car();

    test('Constructor with private property.', function () {
      ok(myCar.color, 'Has a color');
      equal(myCar.gas().mph, 10,
        '.accelerate() should add 10mph.'
      );
      equal(myCar.brake(5).mph, 5,
        '.brake(5) should subtract 5mph.'
      );
      ok(myCar.toggleParkingBrake().isParked(),
        '.toggleParkingBrake works.'
      );
    });
```

You can shave a bit of syntax using the object-literal form:

```
    var myCar = {
      color: 'pink',
      direction: 0,
      mph: 0,

      gas: function gas(amount) {
        amount = amount || 10;
        this.mph += amount;
        return this;
      },

      brake: function brake(amount) {
        amount = amount || 10;
        this.mph = ((this.mph - amount) < 0)? 0
```

```
        : this.mph - amount;
      return this;
    }
};

test('Object literal notation.', function () {
  ok(myCar.color, 'Has a color');

  equal(myCar.gas().mph, 10,
    '.accelerate() should add 10mph.'
  );

  equal(myCar.brake(5).mph, 5,
    '.brake(5) should subtract 5mph.'
  );
});
```

Notice that because the object-literal form doesn't use a function, the encapsulation is gone.

Factories

Object literals have great advantages, but they offer no way to create data privacy. Encapsulation is useful because it hides implementation details from the client. Remember the first principle of OO design from the Gang of Four: "Program to an interface, not an implementation." Encapsulation allows you to enforce that principle in your code, hiding implementation details from the user.

But you already know that constructor functions come with some drawbacks that are best avoided. A better solution is to use a factory method.

A *factory* is a method used to create other objects. Its purpose is to abstract the details of object creation from object use. In object-oriented design, factories are commonly used where a simple class is not enough.

Returning to the singleton example, sometimes it is useful to abstract the singleton reference behind a method call. You can make the singleton instance a private variable and return the reference from a closure:

```
function factory() {
  var highlander = {
      name: 'MacLeod'
    };

  return {
    get: function get() {
      return highlander;
    }
  };
}
```

```
test('Singleton', function () {
  var singleton = factory();
    hero = singleton.get(),
    hero2 = singleton.get();

  hero.sword = 'Katana';

  // Since hero2.sword exists, you know it's the same
  // object.
  ok(hero2.sword, 'There can be only one.');
});
```

You can use the same closure technique to add the parking break functionality to the car:

```
var car = function car(color, direction, mph) {
  var isParkingBrakeOn = false;

  return {
    color: color || 'pink',
    direction: direction || 0,
    mph: mph || 0,
    gas: function gas(amount) {
      amount = amount || 10;
      this.mph += amount;
      return this;
    },

    brake: function brake(amount) {
      amount = amount || 10;
      this.mph = ((this.mph - amount) < 0) ? 0
        : this.mph - amount;
      return this;
    },

    toggleParkingBrake: function toggleParkingBrake() {
      isParkingBrakeOn = !isParkingBrakeOn;
      return this;
    },

    isParked: function isParked() {
      return isParkingBrakeOn;
    }
  };
},
myCar = car('orange', 0, 5);

test('Factory with private variable.', function () {
  ok(myCar.color, 'Has a color');

  equal(myCar.gas().mph, 15,
    '.accelerate() should add 10mph.'
```

```
  );

  equal(myCar.brake(5).mph, 10,
    '.brake(5) should subtract 5mph.'
  );

  ok(myCar.toggleParkingBrake().isParked(),
    '.toggleParkingBrake() toggles on.');

  ok(!myCar.toggleParkingBrake().isParked(),
    '.toggleParkingBrake() toggles off.');
});
```

As with the constructor function, you get data privacy by encapsulating private data inside the closure, so the only way to manipulate the state of the parking brake is through the privileged method: `.toggleParkingBrake()`.

Unlike the constructor function, you don't have to invoke a factory with the new keyword (or worry about forgetting new, or guarding against clobbering the global object inside the function).

Of course, you can also take advantage of prototypes to make the whole thing more efficient:

```
var carPrototype = {
    gas: function gas(amount) {
      amount = amount || 10;
      this.mph += amount;
      return this;
    },
    brake: function brake(amount) {
      amount = amount || 10;
      this.mph = ((this.mph - amount) < 0)? 0
        : this.mph - amount;
      return this;
    },
    color: 'pink',
    direction: 0,
    mph: 0
  },

  car = function car(options) {
    return extend(Object.create(carPrototype), options);
  },

  myCar = car({
    color: 'red'
  });

test('Flyweight factory with cloning', function () {
  ok(Object.getPrototypeOf(myCar).gas,
    'Prototype methods are shared.'
```

```
    );
  });
```

Notice that the factory method itself is now reduced to a one-liner. The arguments list is replaced with an options hash that allows you to specify exactly which values you want to override.

If you take advantage of the prototype feature, you can replace as much or as little of the prototype as you want at runtime. Using the same setup code as before:

```
test('Flyweight factory with cloning', function () {
  // Swap out some prototype defaults:
  extend(carPrototype, {
    name: 'Porsche',
    color: 'black',
    mph: 220
  });

  equal(myCar.name, 'Porsche',
    'Instance inherits the new name.'
  );

  equal(myCar.color, 'red',
    'No instance properties will be impacted.'
  );
});
```

 You should avoid sharing objects and arrays on the prototype if they need to be instance safe. Instead, you can create new copies of the child object/array in the factory.

Prototypal Inheritance with Stamps

JavaScript's object capabilities are really flexible, but Object.create() isn't the easiest way to create a fully featured object. There are still quite a few hoops to jump through just to create a collection of flyweight objects that support data privacy. It gets even more complicated if you want to combine features from more than one source object.

Many libraries provide mechanisms to mimic classical inheritance, but there are few widespread libraries that simplify prototypal object creation, and certainly none that stand out as the gold standard. There is sugar for faking classes coming to JavaScript (I strongly discourage using it). What would it look like if we created sugar for prototypal OO that supported all of the best features JavaScript has to offer?

When thinking about object creation in JavaScript, it helps to ask, what are the important features of objects in JavaScript?

- Delegate prototype
- Instance state
- Encapsulation

A *stamp* is a factory function that has public properties that specify a delegate prototype, default instance state, and a function that sets up encapsulation for object instances. Stamps utilize three different types of inheritance to create the new object:

- Delegate prototype: delegation/differential inheritance
- Instance state: cloning/concatenative inheritance/mixins
- Encapsulation: functional inheritance

Stampit (*https://github.com/dilvie/stampit*) is a library written for this book to demonstrate how we might use sugar to simplify prototypal OO. It exports a single function. Here's the signature:

```
stampit(methods, state, enclose);
```

Here's a more detailed look at how you'd use it to create an object from scratch:

```
var testObj = stampit(
// methods
{
  delegateMethod: function delegateMethod() {
    return 'shared property';
  }
},

// state
{
  instanceProp: 'instance property'
},

// enclose
function () {
  var privateProp = 'private property';

  this.getPrivate = function getPrivate() {
    return privateProp;
  }
}).create();

test('Stampit with params', function () {
  equal(testObj.delegateMethod(), 'shared property',
    'delegate methods should be reachable');

  ok(Object.getPrototypeOf(testObj).delegateMethod,
    'delegate methods should be stored on the ' +
    'delegate prototype');
```

```
    equal(testObj.instanceProp, 'instance property',
      'state should be reachable.');

  ok(testObj.hasOwnProperty('instanceProp'),
    'state should be instance safe.');

  equal(testObj.hasOwnProperty('privateProp'), false,
    'should hide private properties');

  equal(testObj.getPrivate(), 'private property',
    'should support privileged methods');
});
```

Notice that the `.create()` method was called on the returned stamp in order to return the `testObj` instance. The `.create()` method simply returns a new object instance from the stamp. As you can see from the tests, all of the great features that make JavaScript's object system special are available without jumping through all the hoops of setting up your own factory function, figuring out where to store prototypes, and so on.

The stamps returned by `stampit()` also contain methods that can be chained to further define the stamp. This is equivalent to the preceding stamp:

```
var testObj = stampit().methods({
    delegateMethod: function delegateMethod() {
      return 'shared property';
    }
  })
  .state({
    instanceProp: 'instance property'
  })
  .enclose(function () {
    var privateProp = 'private property';

    this.getPrivate = function getPrivate() {
      return privateProp;
    }
  })
  .create();
```

The new object gets created with `Object.create()` using methods as the delegate prototype. Delegate methods are shared among all object instances, which conserve memory resources. If you change a prototype property at runtime, the value change is reflected on every instance of the object. To demonstrate:

```
var stamp = stampit().methods({
    delegateMethod: function delegateMethod() {
      return 'shared property';
    }
  }),
  obj1 = stamp(),
  obj2 = stamp();
```

```
Object.getPrototypeOf(obj1).delegateMethod =
  function () {
    return 'altered';
  };

test('Prototype mutation', function () {
  equal(obj2.delegateMethod(), 'altered',
    'Instances share the delegate prototype.');
});
```

The `.state()` method uses concatenative inheritance, which creates a copy of each property from the state prototypes to the new object, allowing you to safely store instance state. All stamps take an options hash that will be mixed into the instance properties, so it's trivial to initialize a new object:

```
var person = stampit().state({name: ''}),
  jimi = person({name: 'Jimi Hendrix'});


test('Initialization', function () {

  equal(jimi.name, 'Jimi Hendrix',
    'Object should be initialized.');

});
```

The `.enclose()` method uses functional inheritance, which invokes the functions you pass in against the newly created object. You can pass in any number of `.enclose()` functions. Private data will not collide, because a unique closure will be created for each function. Privileged methods will override methods of the same name. Last in wins.

Sometimes it's useful to initialize an object with parameters that don't correspond 1:1 with object properties. The way I prefer to do that is to decouple object instantiation and object initialization. You can do that by creating setters on the object:

```
var person = stampit().enclose(function () {
  var firstName = '',
    lastName = '';

  this.getName = function getName() {
    return firstName + ' ' + lastName;
  };

  this.setName = function setName(options) {
    firstName = options.firstName || '';
    lastName = options.lastName || '';
    return this;
  };
}),

jimi = person().setName({
```

```
    firstName: 'Jimi',
    lastName: 'Hendrix'
});

test('Init method', function () {

equal(jimi.getName(), 'Jimi Hendrix',
    'Object should be initialized.');

});
```

Of course, creating new objects is just scratching the surface of JavaScript's OO capabilities. What you're about to see is not possible with any currently existing popular JavaScript class library. It's not possible with the ES6 class keyword, either.

First, you'll use a closure to create data privacy:

```
var a = stampit().enclose(function () {
  var a = 'a';

  this.getA = function () {
    return a;
  };
});

a().getA(); // 'a'
```

It uses function scope to encapsulate private data. Note that the getter must be defined inside the function in order to access the closure variables. All privileged functions in JavaScript must be defined within the same scope as the private variables they need access to.

And another:

```
var b = stampit().enclose(function () {
  var a = 'b';

  this.getB = function () {
    return a;
  };
});

b().getB(); // 'b'
```

Those a's are not a typo. The point is to demonstrate that a and b's private variables won't clash. Here's where it gets interesting:

```
var c = stampit.compose(a, b),
  foo = c();

foo.getA(); // 'a'
foo.getB(); // 'b'
```

Stampit's `.compose()` method allows you to inherit all three types of prototypes from any number of stamps. The preceding example demonstrates inheritance from multiple ancestors, including private data. Classical OO as we know it today has got nothing on this.

Each stamp has a special property called `fixed`, which stores `methods`, `state`, and `enclose` prototypes. When the stamp is invoked, the `state` prototype is copied so that it is instance safe, the `methods` property is used as the delegate prototype, and each `enclose` function is called in the order in which it was created to set up data privacy (last in wins in the case of name collisions).

The `.compose()` method works a bit like `$.extend()`, but instead of extending objects with the properties of other objects, it extends new objects with the `fixed` prototypes from the factories you pass in, and then calls Stampit and passes them into a new stamp. Like `$.extend()`, `_.extend()`, and so on, last in wins when names collide, which makes it trivial to override stamp features.

Conclusion

Stampit is in production use in web applications with tens of millions of users, so the full source contains several shims for older browsers that enable JavaScript ES5 features. Despite that, it weighs in at about 4 k minified and gzipped. The meat of it is about 90 lines of code (without the shims and comments).

As you can see, JavaScript's object system is flexible and powerful enough to do some really amazing things with very little effort. Imagine how much more fun it could be with a little more built-in language sugar for working with prototypes. `Object.create()` is a good start, but we could do a lot more. By now you should have a whole new respect for prototypes and JavaScript's object system.

Interest in inheritance seems to be waning as Node.js gains popularity. Part of the reason for that is modules. Modules compete with inheritance indirectly but do supply an alternative to inheritance as a code reuse mechanism. Stampit uses Node-style modules to reuse features from a modular utility library. The fact that the library is modular means that Stampit only gets the functionality it needs, and no more. Unlike classical inheritance, modules allow you to pick and choose which features you require.

## CHAPTER 4

Modules

Modules are reusable software components that form the building blocks of applications. Modularity satisfies some very important design goals, perhaps the most important of which is simplicity.

When you design an application with a lot of interdependencies between different parts, it becomes more difficult to fully understand the impact of your changes across the whole system.

If you design parts of a system to a modular interface contract instead, you can safely make changes without having a deep understanding of all of the related modules.

Another important goal of modularity is the ability to reuse your module in other applications. Well-designed modules built on similar frameworks should be easy to transplant into new applications with few (if any) changes. By defining a standard interface for application extensions and then building your functionality on top of that interface, you'll go a long way toward building an application that is easy to extend and maintain and easy to reassemble into different forms in the future.

JavaScript modules are encapsulated, meaning that they keep implementation details private and expose a public API. That way, you can change how a module behaves under the hood without changing code that relies on it. Encapsulation also provides *protection*, meaning that it prevents outside code from interfering with the functionality of the module.

There are several ways to define modules in JavaScript. The most popular and common are the module pattern, CommonJS modules (the inspiration for Node modules), and AMD (Asynchronous Module Definition).

Principles of Modularity

You can think of modules as small, independent applications that are fully functional and fully testable in their own right. Keep them as small and simple as possible to do the job that they are designed to do.

Modules should be:

Specialized

Each module should have a very specific function. The module's parts should be integral to solving the single problem that the module exists to solve. The public API should be simple and clean.

Independent

Modules should know as little as possible about other modules. Instead of calling other modules directly, they should communicate through mediators, such as a central event-handling system or command object.

Decomposable

It should be fairly simple to test and use modules in isolation from other modules. It is common to compare them to components in an entertainment system. You could have a disc player, radio receiver, TV, amplifier, and speakers, all of which can operate independently. If you remove the disc player, the rest of the components continue to function.

Recomposable

It should be possible to fit various modules together in different ways to build a different version of the same software or an entirely different application.

Substitutable

It should be possible to completely substitute one module with another, as long as it supplies the same interface. The rest of the application should not be adversely impacted by the change. The substitute module doesn't have to perform the same function. For example, you might want to substitute a data module that uses REST endpoints as its data source with one that uses a local storage database.

The Open Closed Principle states that a module interface should be open to extension but closed to modification. Changing an interface that a lot of software relies on can be a daunting task. It's best if you can avoid making changes to an existing interface once it has been established. However, software should evolve, and as it does, it should be easy to extend existing interfaces with new functionality.

Interfaces

> Program to an interface, not an implementation.
>
> —The Gang of Four, *Design Patterns*

Interfaces are one of the primary tools of modular software design. Interfaces define a contract that an implementing module will fulfill. For instance, a common problem in JavaScript applications is that the application stops functioning if the Internet connection is lost. In order to solve that problem, you could use local storage and sync changes periodically with the server. Unfortunately, some browsers don't support local storage, so you may have to fall back to cookies or even Flash (depending on how much data you need to store).

Imagine you're writing software that allows users to post notes. You want to store posts in `localStorage` if its available, but fall back to cookie storage if it's not.

That will be difficult if your business logic depends directly on `localStorage` features (see Figure 4-1).

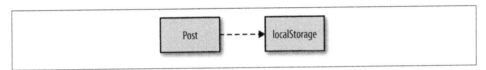

Figure 4-1. Direct dependency

A better alternative is to create a standard interface to provide data access for the post module. That way, the module can save data using the same interface, regardless of where the data is being stored (see Figure 4-2).

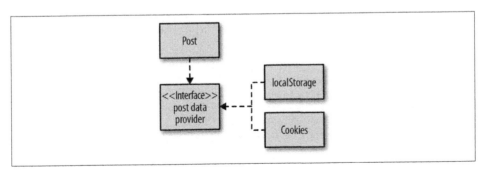

Figure 4-2. Interface

Other languages have native support for interfaces that may enforce the requirements of an interface. You might know them as abstract base classes or pure virtual functions.

In JavaScript, there is no distinction between a class, interface, or object instance. There are only object instances, and that simplification is a good thing. You may be wondering, if there's no native support for interfaces in JavaScript, why bother to write one at all?

When you need multiple implementations of the same interface, it's good to have a canonical reference in the code that explicitly spells out exactly what that interface is. It's important to write code that is self-documenting. For example, a storage interface might have a required `.save()` method. You can write the default implementation so that it will throw if you forget to implement it. Since it's a working prototype, you could even write a sensible default implementation that doesn't throw. In this case, the factory will throw an error if the `.save()` method is not implemented.

Using Stampit to define the factory:

```
(function (exports) {
  'use strict';

  // Make sure local storage is supported.
  var ns = 'post',
    supportsLocalStorage =
      (typeof localStorage !== 'undefined')
        && localStorage !== null,

    storage,

    storageInterface = stampit().methods({
      save: function saveStorage() {
        throw new Error('.save() method not implemented.');
      }
    }),

    localStorageProvider = stampit
      .compose(storageInterface)
      .methods({
        save: function saveLocal() {
          localStorage.storage = JSON.stringify(storage);
        }
      }),

    cookieProvider = stampit
      .compose(storageInterface)
      .methods({
        save: function saveCookie() {
          $.cookie('storage', JSON.stringify(storage));
        }
      }),

    post = stampit().methods({
      save: function save() {
        storage[this.id] = this.data;
        storage.save();
```

```
            return this;
          },
          set: function set(name, value) {
            this.data[name] = value;
            return this;
          }
        })
        .state({
          data: {
            message: '',
            published: false
          },
          id: undefined
        })
        .enclose(function init() {
          this.id = generateUUID();
          return this;
        }),

      api = post;

    storage = (supportsLocalStorage)
      ? localStorageProvider()
      : cookieProvider();

    exports[ns] = api;

}((typeof exports === 'undefined')
      ? window
      : exports
    ));

$(function () {
  'use strict';

  var myPost = post().set('message', 'Hello, world!');

  test('Interface example', function () {
    var storedMessage,
      storage;

    myPost.save();
    storage = JSON.parse(localStorage.storage);
    storedMessage = storage[myPost.id].message;

    equal(storedMessage, 'Hello, world!',
      '.save() method should save post.');
  });
});
```

The important part here is the storage interface. First you create the factory (using Stampit in this case, but it can be any function that returns an object that demonstrates the interface). This example has only one method, `.save()`:

```
storageInterface = stampit().methods({
  save: function saveStorage() {
    throw new Error('.save() method not implemented.');
  }
}),
```

Create a concrete implementation that inherits from the interface. If the interface is especially large, you might want to put each implementation in a separate file. In this case, that isn't required. Notice that the concrete implementations are using named function expressions. During debugging, you'll be able to see which concrete implementation you're using by looking at the function name in the call stack:

```
localStorageProvider = stampit
  .compose(storageInterface)
  .methods({
    save: function saveLocal() {
      localStorage.storage = JSON.stringify(storage);
    }
  }),

cookieProvider = stampit
  .compose(storageInterface)
  .methods({
    save: function saveCookie() {
      $.cookie('storage', JSON.stringify(storage));
    }
  }),
```

Stampit's `.compose()` method allows you to inherit from any number of sources, and it returns a stamp that you can further extend with `.methods()`, `.state()`, or `.en close()`. You can use those features to flesh out the concrete implementations.

The final step is to decide which implementation to use. The following ternary expression checks to see if `localStorage` is supported. If it is, it uses the `localStoragePro vider()`; otherwise, it falls back to cookie storage:

```
storage = (supportsLocalStorage)
  ? localStorageProvider()
  : cookieProvider();
```

There are alternative ways to define interfaces in JavaScript. You could simply define object literals and use something like `jQuery.extend()` to build the desired concrete implementation. The downside there is that you won't be able to take advantage of prototype delegation or data privacy.

You could also define the concrete implementations as prototype objects and then pass the appropriate prototype into Stampit or `Object.create()` during the final step. I prefer to use stamps because they give you a lot of composability.

Erich Gamma, one of the Gang of Four authors who created *Design Patterns*, shared some interesting thoughts about interfaces in an interview with Bill Venners called "Leading-Edge Java Design Principles from Design Patterns: A Conversation with Erich Gamma, Part III" (*http://www.artima.com/lejava/articles/designprinciples.html*).

The Module Pattern

Modules in the browser use a wrapping function to encapsulate private data in a closure (for example, with an IIFE; see "Immediately Invoked Function Expressions" on page 18). Without the encapsulated function scope provided by the IIFE, other scripts could try to use the same variable and function names, which could cause some unexpected behavior.

Most libraries, such as jQuery and Underscore, are encapsulated in modules.

The module pattern encapsulates module contents in an immediately invoked function expression (IIFE) and exposes a public interface by assignment. Douglas Crockford gave the module pattern its name, and Eric Miraglia popularized it in a well-known blog post on the YUI Blog (*http://yuiblog.com/blog/2007/06/12/module-pattern/*).

The original module pattern assigns the result of the IIFE to a predefined namespace variable:

```
var myModule = (function () {
  return {
    hello: function hello() {
      return 'Hello, world!';
    }
  };
}());

test('Module pattern', function () {
  equal(myModule.hello(),
    'Hello, world!',
    'Module works.');
});
```

The problem with this pattern is that you have no choice but to expose at least one global variable for each module. If you're building an application with a lot of modules, that is not a good option. Instead, it's possible to pass in an existing variable to extend with your new module.

Here, that variable is called `exports`, for compatibility with CommonJS (see "Node-Style Modules" on page 82 for an explanation of CommonJS). If `exports` does not exist, you can fall back on `window`:

```
(function (exports) {
  var api = {
      moduleExists: function test() {
        return true;
      }
    };
    $.extend(exports, api);
}((typeof exports === 'undefined') ?
    window : exports));

test('Pass in exports.', function () {
  ok(moduleExists(),
    'The module exists.');
});
```

A common mistake is to pass in a specific application namespace inside your module's source file (instead of using a globally defined `exports`). Normally, that will not harm anything. However, if you wish to reuse the module in another application, you'll have to modify the source of the module in order to attach it to the correct namespace.

Instead, you can pass your application object in as `exports`. It's common in client-side code to have a build step that wraps all of your modules together in a single outer function. If you pass your application object into that wrapper function as a parameter called `exports`, you're in business:

```
var app = {};

(function (exports) {

  (function (exports) {
    var api = {
        moduleExists: function test() {
          return true;
        }
      };
      $.extend(exports, api);
  }((typeof exports === 'undefined') ?
      window : exports));

}(app));

test('Pass app as exports.', function () {
  ok(app.moduleExists(),
    'The module exists.');
});
```

An upside to this version of the module pattern is that the code you write with it can be easily run and tested in Node. From this point on, when the module pattern gets mentioned, this is the version that should spring to mind. Its ancestor is obsolete.

Asynchronous Module Definition

On the client side, there is often a need to load modules asynchronously at runtime in order to avoid the need for the client to download the entire codebase every time the app is loaded. Imagine you have an app like Twitter, where users can post messages or status updates. The core of the application is the messaging feature. However, you also have a large profile editing module that allows users to customize the look of their profile pages.

Users will generally update the look of their profiles a few times per year, so the entire profile editing module (all 50,000 lines of it) goes completely unused 99% of the time. What you need is a way to defer the loading of the profile editor until the user actually enters edit mode. You could just make it a separate page, but then the user has to endure a page refresh, when maybe all she wanted to do was change her profile image. It would be a much better experience to keep this all on one page, with no new page load.

The module pattern doesn't solve this problem. CommonJS modules (like those used by Node) are not asynchronous. In the future, JavaScript will have a native module system that works in the browser (see "ES6 Modules" on page 86), but it's very young technology that may not be widely implemented in all major browsers in the foreseeable future.

AMD is an interim solution to the problem. It works by wrapping the module inside a function called `define()`. The call signature looks like this:

```
define([moduleId,] dependencies, definitionFunction);
```

The `moduleId` parameter is a string that will identify the module. However, this parameter has fallen out of favor because changes in the application or module structure can necessitate a refactor, and there really is no need for an ID in the first place. If you leave it out and begin your define call with the dependency list, you'll create a more adaptable *anonymous module*:

```
define(['ch04/amd1', 'ch04/amd2'],
  function myModule(amd1, amd2) {
    var testResults = {
        test1: amd1.test(),
        test2: amd2.test()
      },

      // Define a public API for your module:
      api = {
        testResults: function () {
          return testResults;
```

```
        }
    };

    return api;
});
```

To kick it off, call `require()`. You specify dependencies similar to `define()`:

```
require(['ch04-amd'], function (amd) {
    var results = amd.testResults();

    test('AMD with Require.js', function () {
        equal(results.test1, true,
            'First dependency loaded correctly.');

        equal(results.test2, true,
            'Second dependency loaded correctly.');
    });
});
```

 Use anonymous modules wherever possible in order to avoid refactors.

The problem with this approach is that if you define your module this way, it can only be used with an AMD loader, such as Require.js or Curl.js (two popular AMD loaders). However, it is possible to get the best of both AMD and module pattern modules. Simply create a module using the module pattern, and at the end of the wrapping function, add this:

```
if (typeof define === 'function') {
    define([], function () {
        return api;
    });
}
```

That way, it will be possible to load your module asynchronously if you want to, but your module will still function properly if it's loaded with a simple `script` tag, or compiled together with a bunch of other modules. This is the pattern that jQuery uses to add AMD loader support. The only trouble with this pattern is that dependency timing is a little more complicated. You'll need to ensure that your dependencies have loaded before you try to use them.

UMD (Universal Module Definition) is another alternative. My favorite way to create a UMD is to bundle the module using Browserify in standalone mode. See "Building Client-Side Code with CommonJS, npm, Grunt, and Browserify" on page 87.

Plug-Ins

Loader plug-ins are an AMD mechanism that allow you to load non-JavaScript resources, such as templates and CSS. Require.js supplies a `text!` plug-in that you can use to load your HTML templates. To use a plug-in, simply prefix the file path with the plug-in name:

```
'use strict';
require(['ch04/mymodule.js', 'text!ch04/mymodule.html'],
    function (myModule, view) {
  var container = document.body,
    css = 'ch04/mymodule.css';

  myModule.render(container, view, css);

  test('AMD Plugins', function () {
    equal($('#mymodule').text(), 'Hello, world!',
      'Plugin loading works.');
  });
});
```

Here's what *mymodule.js* looks like:

```
define(function () {
  'use strict';
  var api = {
    render: function render(container, view, css) {
      loadCss('ch04/mymodule.css');

      $(view).text('Hello, world!')
        .appendTo(container);
    }
  };

  return api;
});
```

And the *mymodule.html* template:

```
<div id="mymodule"></div>
```

The stylesheet is simple:

```
#mymodule {
  font-size:2em;
  color: green;
}
```

Note that the CSS is not loaded as a plug-in. Instead, the URL is assigned to a variable and passed into the `.render()` method for manual loading. The `loadCSS()` function looks like this:

```
function loadCss(url) {
  $('<link>', {
```

```
      type: 'text/css',
      rel: 'stylesheet',
      href: url,
    }).appendTo('head');
}
```

This obviously isn't an ideal solution, but as of this writing, there is no standard rec-ommended `css!` plug-in for Require.js. There is a `css!` plug-in for Curl.js, and you might want to try Xstyle. Use them the same way you define the HTML template.

AMD has a couple of serious drawbacks. First, it requires you to include a boilerplate wrapper function for every module. Second, it forces you to either compile your whole application in a compile step, or asynchronously load every single module on the client side, which, in spite of advertising to the contrary, could actually slow down the load and execution of your scripts due to simultaneous download limits and connection latency.

I recommend the precompile solution over the asynchronous load solution, and as long as you're doing that anyway, you may as well be using the simplified CommonJS syntax and a tool like Browserify (*http://browserify.org/*). See "Building Client-Side Code with CommonJS, npm, Grunt, and Browserify" on page 87.

Node-Style Modules

CommonJS is a set of standards for JavaScript environments that attempts to make JavaScript engine implementations more compatible. CommonJS modules specify an API that modules use to declare dependencies. CommonJS module implementations are responsible for reading the modules and resolving those dependencies.

Before Node.js, there were several other attempts to run JavaScript on the server side, as far back as the late 1990s. Both Netscape and Microsoft allowed JavaScript-compatible scripting in their server environments. However, few people used those capabilities. The first server-side JavaScript solution to gain any real traction was Rhino, but it was too slow and cumbersome to build web-scale applications on top of.

By the time Node.js arrived on the scene, there were several different server-side envi-ronments for JavaScript that all started out using different conventions for dealing with issues such as module loading. CommonJS was created to solve that problem. Node-style modules are essentially an implementation of the CommonJS module specification.

The CommonJS module system has a much simpler syntax than either the module pattern or AMD. In CommonJS, the file is the module. There is no need for a function wrapper to contain the scope, because each file is given its own scope. Modules declare dependencies with a synchronous `require()` function. That means that execution is blocked while the required module is being resolved, so it's safe to start using the module immediately after you require it.

First, assign to keys on the free variable `exports` to declare your module's public API:

```
'use strict';
var foo = function foo () {
  return true;
};

exports.foo = foo;
```

Then use `require()` to import your module and assign it to a local variable. You can specify the name of a module in the list of installed Node modules or specify a path to the module using relative paths.

For example, if you want to use the Flatiron HTTP module, you can `require()` by name (from the Flatiron.js (*http://flatironjs.org/#routing*) docs):

```
var flatiron = require('flatiron'),
  app = flatiron.app;

app.use(flatiron.plugins.http, {
  // HTTP options
});

//
// app.router is now available. app[HTTP-VERB] is also available
// as a shortcut for creating routes
//
app.router.get('/version', function () {
  this.res.writeHead(200, { 'Content-Type': 'text/plain' })
  this.res.end('flatiron ' + flatiron.version);
});

app.start(8080);
```

Or specify a relative path:

```
'use strict';
var mod = require('./ch04-modules.js'),
  result = (mod.foo() === true) ? 'Pass:' : 'Fail:';

console.log(result, '.foo() should return true.');
```

Here, `console.log()` is used to simulate a unit testing framework, but there are several better alternatives for Node, including tape (*https://github.com/substack/tape*) and nodeunit (*https://github.com/caolan/nodeunit*).

npm

Node package manager (npm) is a package manager that comes bundled with Node. Contrary to popular belief, npm is not an acronym (*https://www.npmjs.org/doc/faq.html*), according to the npm FAQ, so it's technically incorrect to capitalize the letters. It provides an easy way to install modules for your application, including all required dependencies. Node relies on the *package.json* specification for package configuration. It's common to use npm to pull in all of your project's dependencies on the server side, but there is also a movement forming to use npm to pull in dependencies for the client side as well.

npm has a number of well-documented directives, but for the purposes of this book, you'll only need to know the ones you'll commonly need to modify in order to get your typical app up and running:

name
> The name of the package.

version
> Package version number (npm modules must use semantic versioning).

author
> Some information about the author.

description
> A short description of the package.

keywords
> Search terms to help users find the package.

main
> The path of the main package file.

scripts
> A list of scripts to expose to npm; most projects should define a "test" script that runs with the command npm test, which you can use to execute your unit tests.

repository
> The location of the package repository.

dependencies, bundledDependencies
> Dependencies your package will require().

devDependencies
> A list of dependencies that developers will need in order to contribute.

engines
> Specifies which version of Node to use.

If you want to build a Node app, one of the first things you'll need to do is create a server. One of the easiest ways to do that is to use Express, a minimal application framework for Node. Before you begin, you should look at the latest version available. By the time you read this, the version you see here should no longer be the latest:

$ npm info express

```
3.0.0rc5
```

Example 4-1 shows how to add it to your *package.json* file.

Example 4-1. package.json

```json
{
  "name": "simple-express-static-server",
  "version": "0.1.0",
  "author": "Sandro Padin",
  "description": "A very simple static file server. For development use only.",
  "keywords": ["http", "web server", "static server"],
  "main": "./server.js",
  "scripts": {
    "start": "node ./server.js"
  },
  "repository": {
    "type": "git",
    "url": "https://github.com/spadin/simple-express-static-server.git"
  },
  "dependencies": {
    "express": "3.0.x"
  },
  "engines": {
    "node": ">=0.6"
  }
}
```

Notice that the Express version is specified as 3.0.x. The x acts like a wildcard. It will install the latest 3.0 version, regardless of the patch number. It's another way of saying, "give me bug fixes, but no API changes." Node modules use semantic versioning (*http://semver.org/*). Read it as Major.Minor.Patch. Working backward, bug fixes increment the patch version, nonbreaking API changes increment the minor version, and backward-breaking changes increment the major version. A zero for the major version indicates initial development. The public API should not be considered stable, and there is no indication in the version string for backward-breaking changes.

Now that your package and dependencies are declared, return to the console and run:

$ npm install

```
express@3.0.0rc5 node_modules/express
├── methods@0.0.1
├── fresh@0.1.0
```

```
├── range-parser@0.0.4
├── cookie@0.0.4
├── crc@0.2.0
├── commander@0.6.1
├── debug@0.7.0
├── mkdirp@0.3.3
├── send@0.1.0 (mime@1.2.6)
└── connect@2.5.0 (pause@0.0.1, bytes@0.1.0, send@0.0.4, formidable@1.0.11,
    qs@0.5.1)
```

When you run npm install, it will look at *package.json* and install all of the dependencies for you, including those that were declared by the express package.

ES6 Modules

None of the module systems discussed so far are included in the official ECMAScript specifications. In the future, a module system will be built in to all ECMA-compliant JavaScript engines.

The ES6 module specification isn't widely usable yet, but when it is, it should be possible to write modules and compile using build tools to fall back on the module pattern, AMD, and CommonJS where required. ES6 module build tools are already beginning to appear, but you should probably wait a bit longer before you start to rely on them for your production applications.

ES6 modules are similar to Node modules, with subtle differences. Instead of mod ule.exports, you get the export keyword:

```
var foo = function foo () {
  return true;
};

export { foo };
```

Instead of require(), there's a new import keyword:

```
import { foo } from 'es6-foo';

let test = foo() === true ? 'Pass' : 'Fail';

console.log(test, 'foo() should import and return true.');
```

In both cases, you can include multiple variables inside the import/export brackets, but I recommend that you try to export one thing from each module. Keep it simple. You can also rename the imported variable using the keyword as:

```
import { foo as bar } from 'es6-foo';
```

When you're only exporting one thing, you should make it the default export:

```
var foo = function foo () {
  return true;
```

```
};

    export default foo; // No braces required
```

Now you can use the simplified import:

```
    import foo from 'es6-foo'; // No braces required
```

If you are interested in experimenting with ES6 modules today, you can use them with the Browserify transform, es6ify (*https://github.com/thlorenz/es6ify*).

Building Client-Side Code with CommonJS, npm, Grunt, and Browserify

There are a variety of competing standards for module management with JavaScript, but due to the popularity of Node, by far the most established is npm + CommonJS. There have been efforts to create a similar combination of features for the client side, including AMD, Yeoman (*http://yeoman.io/*), and Bower (*http://bower.io/*), but none of them can compete with the simplicity and package availability of npm and CommonJS modules.

To demonstrate, take a look at how you might build a minimal client-side guest-list app (just in case you need a bouncer at your birthday party).

Defining the App

Most new software projects use agile development methods to produce quick software creation and enhancement iterations. In agile software, the time between releases is measured in days or weeks rather than months or years. To learn more about agile, see *The Art of Agile Development: Pragmatic guide to agile software development* by James Shore (O'Reilly, 2007).

Typically when you set out to build an app, you'll start with a list of *user stories*. You can use those scenarios to come up with *acceptance criteria*, which can be further distilled into functional unit tests.

A user story is a short, simple description of some action that your user might want to perform. For example, "As an event organizer, I want to check arriving guests against the guest list." User stories should always contain a role along with the story. Answer the questions, "Who is performing the action?" and "What is the user trying to accomplish?"

To express this example story in code, you'll need a list element with clickable links in list items. The unit tests might look something like Example 4-2.

Example 4-2. guestlist/test/test.js

```javascript
var $list = $('#guestlist-view'),
  checkedinClass = 'icon-check',
  guestSelector = '.guest';

test('Guestlist', function () {
  ok($list.length,
    'List element should have guests.');
});

test('Guests', function () {

  // Grab the first guest from the list
  var $guest = $($list.find(guestSelector)[0]),
    guestExists = !!$guest[0];

  // Simulate click
  $guest.click();

  ok($guest.hasClass(checkedinClass),
      'Should be checked on click');

  $guest.click();

  // To avoid a false positive, make sure
  // you have a guest element to test against.
  ok(guestExists && !$guest.hasClass(checkedinClass),
      'Should toggle off when clicked again');
});
```

You'll need to include that in your QUnit HTML file, as shown in Example 4-3.

Example 4-3. guestlist/test/index.html

```html
<!DOCTYPE html>
  <html>
    <head>
    </head>
    <body>
      <section>
        <h1 id="qunit-header">QUnit Test Suite</h1>
        <h2 id="qunit-banner"></h2>
        <div id="qunit-testrunner-toolbar"></div>
        <h2 id="qunit-userAgent"></h2>
        <ol id="qunit-tests"></ol>
      </section>

      <section id="container"></section>

      <script src="jquery.js"></script>
      <script src="qunit.js"></script>
      <script src="../public/app.js"></script>
```

```
<script src="test.js"></script>
<link href="qunit.css" rel="stylesheet"></style>

  </body>
</html>
```

These tests will obviously fail at first. That's a good thing. If you can see your tests fail before you make them pass, you eliminate the possibility that your test results are showing you false positives. For this reason, *TDD* (test-driven development) proponents advocate writing your unit tests before you implement the code that they're written against. Because you're writing from an API user perspective when you write tests first, using test-driven development forces you to write more modular, testable code. You may also notice that your APIs are easier to use because you're not worried about implementation details when you write your tests—you won't accidentally leak implementation details into your APIs.

In fact, while I was writing this example, I started with the preceding tests, and then decided to implement the features. I was tempted to use some Twitter Bootstrap controls out of the box to implement my styles, but that would have forced me to expose unnecessary markup details in the API because Bootstrap makes assumptions about the tags you'll use to implement controls. As a result, I adapted the stylesheet to pass the tests, and the API is better for it. Had I not written failing tests first, I might have accepted the extra markup, overcomplicated the example, and then written tests that passed against the inferior implementation.

 Twitter Bootstrap is a popular CSS framework that is sometimes useful for prototyping web applications quickly. It's a good idea to play with it and see if it would be useful to you. Remember, though, that it's designed to be tweaked and customized. Don't feel like you have to conform to the default markup and classes if they don't fit your particular use case.

There's a running joke about how many sites look the same because they use all the same Bootstrap styles and controls. You may want to mix it up a little. There's an interesting blog post on the topic called "Customize Twitter Bootstrap To Not Look Bootstrap-y" by Antonin Januska (*http://bit.ly/1pFHYAl*).

Time to see the test output from QUnit, shown in Figure 4-3.

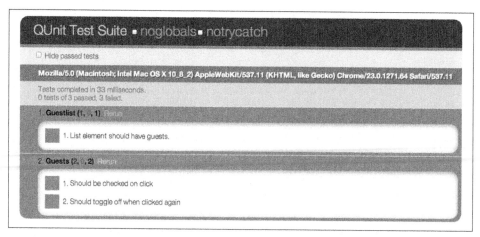

Figure 4-3. Failing QUnit screenshot

Feature Implementation

Failing tests will be listed in red. To make the tests turn green, you'll need to implement the features. Normally, it's wise to break the code up into separate concerns. There's a lot more on that topic in Chapter 5. In this case, you'll separate presentation concerns from data management. The data will come from a stubbed model module named *guestlistmodel.js*. For now, it will just return some hard-coded names. You can implement loading and saving later, as shown in Example 4-4.

Example 4-4. guestlist/src/guestlistmodel.js

```
var api = {
    load: function load() {
      return [
        'Jimi Hendrix',
        'Billie Holiday',
        'Nina Simone',
        'Jim Morrison',
        'Duke Ellington',
        'John Bonham'
      ];
    }
  };

module.exports = api;
```

As you can see, this file is pretty straightforward. It just defines an `api` object and sets it on `module.exports` to expose it to other modules in accordance with the CommonJS specification.

The code to manipulate the list DOM elements will go into a file named *guestlist-view.js*, as shown in Example 4-5.

Example 4-5. guestlist/src/guestlistview.js

```
var $ = require('jquery-browserify'),
  checkedinClass = 'icon-check',
  listClass = 'dropdown-menu',
  guestClass = 'guest',

  toggleCheckedIn = function toggleCheckedIn(e) {
    $(this).toggleClass(checkedinClass);
  },

  $listView = $('<ol>', {
    id: 'guestlist-view',
    'class': listClass
  }).on('click', '.' + guestClass, toggleCheckedIn),

  render = function render(guestlist) {

    $listView.empty();

    guestlist.forEach(function (guest) {
      $guest = $('<li class="' + guestClass + '">' +
        '<span class="name">' + guest +
        '</span></li>');
      $guest.appendTo($listView);
    });

    return $listView;
  },

  api = {
    render: render
  };

module.exports = api;
```

This is the file doing all the work. First, it uses `.require()` to get a reference to jQuery and sets a few self-documenting variable names. The `toggleCheckedIn()` function is an event handler for the `click` event.

The list element gets added. Note that it's using jQuery's `.on()` method to delegate the click events. `.on()` is the recently recommended way to hook up event handlers in jQuery. It replaces the deprecated `.bind()`, `.live()`, and `.delegate()` methods with a simplified syntax and more consistent signature.

By delegating to the parent-ordered list element, you can replace, remove, and add children to the list without worrying about removing and replacing event listeners. There won't be any memory leaks, and you don't have to wait until the whole list is rendered before you attach the listener. If you're hooking up listeners to DOM elements, most of the time, delegating to an ancestor is the right approach.

The `.render()` method takes an array of guest names, iterates over each one, and adds a corresponding list item to the `$listView` element. It then returns the rendered element to the calling function.

The rest of the code simply defines the public API and exposes it via CommonJS.

Some developers will intersperse `module.exports` assignments throughout a module. I find that having a single `module.exports` at the bottom of the file more clearly documents the module's public API.

So far, the modules don't know about each other, so there's no way for them to do any work. To bring all the pieces together and manage the initial render, you'll need a higher level abstraction to kick things off. Enter *app.js*, as shown in Example 4-6.

Example 4-6. guestlist/src/app.js

```
var $ = require('jquery-browserify'),
  guestlistModel = require('./guestlistmodel'),
  guestlistView = require('./guestlistview'),
  $container = $('#container');

$(function init() {
  var guestlistData = guestlistModel.load();
    $guestlist = guestlistView.render(guestlistData);
  $container.empty().append($guestlist);
});
```

This one should be fairly simple to follow. It uses `require()` to reference `guestlistMo del` and `guestlistView`, loads the guestlist, passes the data into `guestlistView.ren der()`, and adds it to the `container` element.

The `.append()` line at the end of the `init()` function calls jQuery's `.empty()` method first for a couple of important reasons. First, if there's anything in that space already, it should be replaced, but it also releases references to event listeners so that the memory can be garbage collected. This is a better strategy than simply calling `.html()`. The latter is by far the more popular method, but it can be a major source of bugs and confusion when you start to develop large, client-heavy applications in JavaScript.

Bundling and Deployment

None of this is going to work yet, because the modules all need to be compiled together in order of their dependencies. For that, you'll need Browserify.

Browserify (*https://github.com/substack/node-browserify*) is a Node module that makes CommonJS modules work in the browser, using a server-side build step. The `browser ify` command is available to kick off the bundle:

```
$ browserify src/app.js -o public/app.js
```

That's a bit too manual, though. You'll want to use `grunt` to automate the build. That way you can lint, build, and run your unit tests all in one step. Start with *package.json*, as shown in Example 4-7.

Example 4-7. guestlist/package.json

```json
{
  "name": "guestlist",
  "version": "0.1.0",
  "author": "Eric Elliott",
  "description": "A handy tool for bouncers.",
  "keywords": ["party", "guestlist"],
  "main": "dist/app.js",
  "scripts": {
    "test": "grunt test"
  },
  "dependencies": {
    "jquery-browserify": "*"
  },
  "devDependencies": {
    "traverse": "*",
    "grunt": "*",
    "grunt-browserify": "*",
    "browserify": "*"
  },
  "engines": {
    "node": ">=0.6"
  }
}
```

Since you'll be deploying this app, you should consider all of the code it uses to be part of the app, including its dependencies. You don't want those dependency versions shifting around under your feet during your deploy step. The less uncertainty and moving parts you have in a deploy step the better. For that reason, you're going to want to check in your `node_modules` directory (don't add it to `.gitignore`).

Because all of the dependencies are going to be checked into the repository, you don't need to specify the versions to install. The "*" indicates that you want to use the latest version. This practice assumes that you have been religiously unit testing your code, that your deploy does not require its own `npm install` (which I strongly discourage), and that you block deploys when integration tests fail. In other words, * allows you to keep up with the latest versions, but if you plan to use it, you need to have a process in place so that you don't break your production deployment if something changes.

You'll also need a gruntfile. Older versions of Grunt look for *grunt.js* by default. Versions after 0.4.0 expect *gruntfile.js*, instead (see Example 4-8).

Example 4-8. guestlist/grunt.js

```
/*global module*/
module.exports = function(grunt) {
  'use strict';
  grunt.initConfig({

    // Read package.json into an object for later
    // reference (for example, in meta, below).
    pkg: '<json:package.json>',

    meta: {

      // A template to add to the top of the bundled
      // output.
      banner: '\n/*! <%= pkg.title || pkg.name %> ' +
        '- v<%= pkg.version %> - ' +
        '<%= grunt.template.today("yyyy-mm-dd") %>\n ' +
        '<%= pkg.homepage ? "* " + pkg.homepage + "\n' +
        ' *\n " : "" %>' +
        '* Copyright (c) ' +
        '<%= grunt.template.today("yyyy") %> ' +
        '<%= pkg.author.name %>;\n' +
        ' * Licensed under the <%= ' +
        '_.pluck(pkg.licenses, "type").join(", ") %>' +
        ' license */'
    },

    // Specify which files to send through JSHint.
    lint: {
      all: ['./grunt.js', './src/**/*.js',
        './test-src/test.js']
    },
```

```javascript
  // JSHint configuration options.
  jshint: {
    browser: false,
    node: true,
    strict: false,
    curly: true,
    eqeqeq: true,
    immed: true,
    latedef: true,
    newcap: true,
    nonew: true,
    noarg: true,
    sub: true,
    undef: true,
    unused: true,
    eqnull: true,
    boss: false
  },

  // Specify test locations for QUnit.
  qunit: {
    browser: ['test/index.html']
  },

  // Configuration for browserify.
  browserify: {
    "public/app.js": {
      requires: ['traverse'],
      entries: ['src/**/*.js'],
      prepend: ['<banner:meta.banner>'],
      append: [],
      hook: function () {
        // bundle is passed in as first param
      }
    }
  }

});

// Load browserify tasks. Needed for bundling.
grunt.loadNpmTasks('grunt-browserify');

// Setup command line argument tasks. For e.g.:
// $ grunt # executes lint, browserify, qunit
// $ grunt test # runs qunit task, only.
grunt.registerTask('default', 'lint browserify qunit');
grunt.registerTask('install', 'browserify');
grunt.registerTask('test', 'qunit');
};
```

The Grunt configuration file is just a Node JavaScript module, so you can write functions in it, evaluate expressions, and so on.

Browserify requires a little extra configuration sometimes. Please refer to the grunt-browserify documentation (*https://github.com/pix/grunt-browserify*) for specific settings. Just don't forget to load the grunt tasks with grunt.loadNpmTasks('grunt-browserify').

The .registerTask() calls make grunt command-line arguments available. For example, all the default tasks will run when you execute grunt without any arguments, and grunt test will only run the tests.

Time for some action:

```
$ grunt
Running "lint:all" (lint) task
Lint free.

Running "browserify:public/app.js" (browserify) task

Running "qunit:browser" (qunit) task
Testing index.html..OK
>> 3 assertions passed (32ms)

Done, without errors.
```

Notice the QUnit task output. The tests are green, and in this form, you can run them on an automated continuous integration system.

In case you're curious, Figure 4-4 shows the browser output.

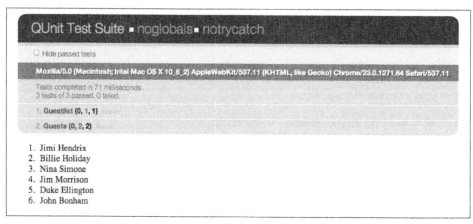

Figure 4-4. Passing QUnit screenshot

In general, CSS is a little outside the scope of this book, but there are a few tips you should be aware of. For some great ideas on how to use CSS for applications, see "Scalable and Modular Architecture for CSS" by Jonathan Snook (*http://smacss.com/*).

The Guestlist code employs a custom icon font for the checkbox. Fonts provide a major advantage over traditional methods like png icons. For instance, they are infinitely scaleable, and you can apply any CSS you'd normally apply to text. You can also create a single, custom font that is easy for clients to download. The font was created using a free custom font app called IcoMoon (*http://icomoon.io/*). Example 4-9 shows the icon font-related CSS.

Example 4-9. Icon font CSS

```
@font-face {
  font-family: 'guestlist';
  src:url('fonts/guestlist.eot');
  src:url('fonts/guestlist.eot?#iefix')
      format('embedded-opentype'),
    url('fonts/guestlist.svg#guestlist')
      format('svg'),
    url('fonts/guestlist.woff') format('woff'),
    url('fonts/guestlist.ttf') format('truetype');
  font-weight: normal;
  font-style: normal;
}

[class^="icon-check"]:before,
[class*=" icon-check"]:before {
  font-family: 'guestlist';
  font-style: normal;
  font-size: .75em;
  speak: none;
  font-weight: normal;
  -webkit-font-smoothing: antialiased;
}
.icon-check:before {
  content: "\e000";
}
.dropdown-menu .icon-check .name {
  padding-left: 1em;
}
```

Conclusion

By now you should be familiar with the concept of modularity and comfortable with the idea of using build tools to bundle your application for deployment. You've seen an example of how to do that with Browserify. You should be able to figure out how to accomplish the same thing with AMD, if that's your preference.

You saw some hinting at separation of concerns in this chapter, splitting the model from the view and so on. In the next chapter, you'll see a much deeper explanation of what that means.

## CHAPTER 5

Separation of Concerns

Separation of concerns is the idea that each module or layer in an application should only be responsible for one thing and should not contain code that deals with other things. Separating concerns reduces code complexity by breaking a large application down into many smaller units of encapsulated functionality.

It's easy to confuse separation of concerns with employing modules for the construction of your application, but separation of concerns also implies the layering of functionality in your application. For example, n-tier architecture and MVC architectures are the result of separating concerns across the entire application, rather than at the individual module level. The goal of MVC and related patterns is to separate data management from presentation.

Separation of concerns can be expressed as functions, modules, controls, widgets, layers, tiers, services, and so on. The various units of concern vary from one app to the next, and each different app may use a different combination. Functions and modules have already been discussed.

A *control* is a reusable GUI input that enables user interaction with your application. For example, combo boxes, calendar inputs, sliders, buttons, switches, and knobs are all controls.

A *widget* is a small application which is intended to be embedded in other applications. For example, WordPress (*http://wordpress.org/*) allows developers to offer embeddable units of functionality to blog owners through its plug-in ecosystem. There are many widgets to manage calendars, comments, maps, and all sorts of services from third-party providers.

The word widget is historically used to mean the same thing as controls. To avoid confusion, this book will always refer to interactive form inputs as controls (or inputs), and widgets will always refer to embeddable mini applications.

Layers are logical groupings of functionality. For example, a data layer might encapsulate functionality related to data and state, while a presentation layer handles display concerns, such as rendering to the DOM and binding UI behaviors.

Tiers are the runtime environments that layers get deployed to. A runtime environment usually consists of at least one physical computer, an operating system, the runtime engine (e.g., Node, Java, or Ruby), and any configuration needed to express how the application should interact with its environment.

It's possible to run multiple layers on the same tier, but tiers should be kept independent enough that they can easily be deployed to separate machines or even separate data centers. For large-scale applications, it's usually also necessary that tiers can scale horizontally, meaning that as demand increases, you can add machines to a tier in order to improve its capacity to meet that demand.

Client-Side Concerns

There are several client-side concerns that almost every mature JavaScript application might deal with at some point:

- Module management
- Events
- Presentation and DOM manipulation
- Internationalization
- Data management and IO (including Ajax)
- Routing (translating URLs to script actions)
- Logging
- Analytics tracking
- Authentication
- Feature toggling (decouple code deployment and feature release)

Various libraries and frameworks exist that generally attempt to provide some combination of mechanisms to deal with these concerns. Libraries roughly fall into two categories: minimal and monolithic. Minimal libraries generally provide a handful of objects and methods which make it easier to build well organized applications. Perhaps the most famous example is Backbone.js, which provides views, models, collections, routers, and events.

That may sound like a lot, until you compare it to something like the Dojo framework, which is something like a library of libraries. It includes an impressive array of components that do everything from extending JavaScript with ideas from other programming languages, like aspects (aspect-oriented programming), to DOM widgets, such as a calendar. Dojo is interesting because it started out more monolithic, and now it's actually a tiny module loader with a large library of components that you can use if you wish, without loading the entire Dojo framework.

Larger frameworks tend to be more heavy-handed (opinionated) about how your application architecture should function.

There is a growing trend in the JavaScript community moving in the direction of microlibraries, and microlibrary frameworks. Microjs.com (*http://microjs.com/*) has a list of interesting microlibraries. You should certainly explore the wealth of microlibraries available in the community and use the ones that solve your problems.

You might see microlibrary proponents discourage the use of jQuery, not least because it's quite large compared to most microlibraries. However, there is some security in using a well-tested library like jQuery because it is used and improved by thousands of other smart developers. It's usually safe to assume that jQuery will mostly behave as expected (of course, there are always exceptions).

Despite the claims of microlibary authors, most microlibraries have not undergone the same level of scrutiny as jQuery, and small libraries don't equate to bug-free libraries. Everybody makes mistakes. Be prepared to debug them as you work with them. Please contribute fixes back to the author if you find and fix a bug.

It's also likely that you'll use most of jQuery's core feature set in every application that you build. I see no good reason to reassemble that feature set from microlibraries every time you start a new project.

Also be aware that many microlibraries may need to reinvent the wheel over and over again for commonly needed patterns, like copying attributes from one object to another (as in jQuery or Underscore's `.extend()` method). It might seem like a good idea to use less code, but there's a chance you'll end up using more, instead, unless you go with a well-organized microlibrary framework with components designed to be used together.

In order to decide which application frameworks or libraries might help you build your application, take a look at the TodoMVC project (*http://todomvc.com/*), which compares many commonly used libraries, such as Backbone.js, Angular.js, Dojo, and YUI, by showing you an example of what a simple Todo application looks like using each library.

Module Management

Module management is concerned with supplying a standard architecture that allows your modules to fit together easily and communicate with each other without being tightly coupled.

The module manager prescribes a standard module API that all other modules can implement and a sandbox of common library functionality that any module can use so that application modules can stay lightweight and focus exclusively on the service that they provide.

Module management typically supplies your application with:

- Namespacing
- Sandbox (a base layer of functionality that other modules can safely use)
- Access to environment variables and bootstrapped data
- Module lifecycle hooks (help with setup and teardown)
- An event system for inter-module communication

Nicholas Zakas gave a related talk called Scalable JavaScript Application Architecture (*http://slidesha.re/1pFIYUQ*), and Addy Osmani (author of Aura) wrote about it in Patterns For Large-Scale JavaScript Application Architecture (*http://addyosmani.com/largescalejavascript/*). Often, module-management implementations are part of a monolithic application library tightly coupled to a proprietary codebase, or both.

Aura is a good example of an open-source implementation with a fairly narrow focus on module management—with one clear difference: Aura has a strong focus on UI components, which are modules that have UI elements that need to be rendered to the screen. A generic module could perform any type of service and may or may not need a dedicated space to render. A component exists primarily for the purpose of supplying UI output or UI interaction.

For the sake of clarity and simplicity in the following examples, I wrote a simple module management solution called Tinyapp. It is an open source library. To get the source, clone it from GitHub:

```
$ git clone git://github.com/dilvie/tinyapp.git
```

Getting started

As of this writing, Tinyapp is rapidly evolving. Please see the Tinyapp website (*http://tinyappjs.com/*) to learn how to download and install the latest version.

Simply `require()` it and initialize your app:

```
var app = require('tinyapp');
```

```
app.init({
  environment: environment,
  pageData: pageData,
  beforeRender: [promise1, promise2...]
});
```

The `environment` object (optional) is the primary means of passing application environment configuration into your JavaScript application. Use it for passing in data that usually has to come from server-side configuration, such as environment domain names, application IDs for third-party services, CDN URLs, etc.

There are a couple of ways you could source the environment from the server side: load it with Ajax or include it in the HTML with an inline script.

The `pageData` object is intended to register bootstrapped data with the app at page-load time.

`beforeRender` is a list of promises that all must finish before the render phase begins. For example, many apps will need i18n translations to load before any module is allowed to render. By adding an i18n promise to the application's `beforeRender` queue, you can postpone render until the translations are loaded. Using `beforeRender` can prevent tricky race condition bugs and provide a neat solution if you need a guaranteed way to handle tasks before the modules render. See "Registration, loading, and rendering" on page 104 for more about application and module timing hooks.

> Be careful with the global `beforeRender` queue. Each item you add to it compounds the possibility that something in the queue will fail, which might significantly delay or block the render of your application. If what you're waiting for only impacts a single module, keep the waiting logic isolated to that module.

Here's how you might build up a typical Tinyapp module:

1. Require Tinyapp:

   ```
   var app = require('tinyapp');
   ```

2. Provide an API:

   ```
   var app = require('tinyapp'),

     hello = function hello() {
       return 'hello, world';
     },

     api = {
       hello: hello
     };
   ```

3. Export your module:

```
var app = require('tinyapp'),

  hello = function hello() {
    return 'hello, world';
  },

  api = {
    hello: hello
  };

module.exports = api;
```

 This contrived example should really be simplified even further. Since it doesn't actually use tinyapp, it doesn't need to require it, and since it's only exporting a single function (which is actually a pretty good idea for lots of modules), it could just be module.exports = func tion hello() { ...

Any standard node-style module could be used as a Tinyapp module, but as you'll see, Tinyapp provides some utility and benefit that you'll use a lot.

Registration, loading, and rendering

If you need to fetch some data asynchronously before you render your module, Tinyapp helps speed things up by launching your asynchronous calls as early as possible.

Module initialization is broken into two phases: load and render. Imagine you want to asynchronously fetch some data while the page is still loading so that you can begin to render it as early as possible. This can speed up your perceived page-load times.

The solution is to kick off the asynchronous fetch at load time so that it begins the download as early as possible: before the DOM is ready, and before the page is done processing all the HTML, CSS, and JavaScript. Since the load is asynchronous, it will introduce only a few milliseconds of latency during the load phase, but it'll do most of the work in the background while the browser continues processing the rest of the page in parallel with the load.

If you have data that is secondary to the main purpose of the page, and you can get away with waiting until after the DOM is ready, it's a good idea to let your page load normally and fetch the data during the render step, instead of using the early load hook. This will reduce the number of page requests that must be handled at page-load time (eliminating the latency hit) and hopefully also improve the perceived performance of your app.

Tinyapp allows you to hook into those page-load phases individually so you can optimize page-load times and manage render dependencies without worrying about asynchronous timing issues.

You can specify load() and render() callbacks by passing them into a registration method:

```
app.register({
  load: load,
  render: render
});
```

The render() callback is called after:

- Any promise returned by load() is resolved. For example, if you return a jQuery Ajax promise from your load() function, it will wait until the Ajax fetch is complete. All jQuery Ajax calls return compatible promises.
- All beforeRender callbacks have fired (see "Getting started" on page 102).
- The DOM is ready to be manipulated.

Registration is optional. If you don't need any of the features it provides, you aren't required to use it.

Time for an example. Imagine you have a widget that displays tour dates for bands. Here's how it could work:

```
var
  app = require('tinyapp'),
  view = require('./view'),
  data,

  load = function load() {
    var url = 'http://api.bandsintown.com/artists/' +
      'Skrillex.json?api_version=2.0&amp;app_id=YOUR_APP_ID';

    whenLoaded = app.get(url);
    whenLoaded.done(function (response) {
      data = response;
    });

    return whenLoaded.promise();
  },

  render = function render() {
    view.render(data);
  };

app.register({
  load: load,
  render: render,
});

module.exports = api;
```

Try not to do anything blocking in your load() function. For example, you might want to fetch the data that you need to complete your page render, but if you're loading a large collection and you need to iterate over the collection and do some data processing, save the data processing step for render() time, when you're not blocking the page render process.

It's not safe to manipulate the DOM at all in your load() function.

Events

Events are a method of communicating between different application modules or components in order to achieve loose coupling, asynchronous communication, interprocess communication, or any combination of the above. For example, the browser environment is event driven. It presents DOM elements to users (buttons and form inputs, for example), and then responds to user input by firing events for the application to listen for and handle.

You're probably already familiar with responding to existing browser DOM events. If you need a refresher, consult the Mozilla DOM Reference (*https://developer.mozilla.org/en-US/docs/DOM*). This section covers defining and using your own custom events, independent of the DOM.

In order to keep modules decoupled from each other, it's helpful to think of events as reports of what has happened, rather than commands for what should happen next. Other modules can listen for the events they care about and decide what to do next on their own.

Event emitters

Often we need to provide a method API that can handle a range of asynchronous communication. A good solution to this problem is to return an object that emits events. DOM elements are event emitters, so that they can notify you of user input or other state changes. For example, most elements emit a click event when the user clicks them, and the HTML5 video API emits events for loading progress, playback position changes, and a variety of other information that isn't immediately known.

It's possible to create your own event emitter API that you can mix into any JavaScript object. A minimal implementation might only have three methods: .on(), .trigger(), and .off().

Backbone.js is a client-side MV* library that provides event emitters for models, views, routers, and collections. If you're using Backbone (which relies on Underscore), you can turn any object into an event emitter like this:

```
_.extend(myObject, Backbone.Events);

myObject.on('my_event', function handle(data) {
  console.log(data);
});

object.trigger('my_event', 'hi'); // logs 'hi'
```

The downside to triggering events only on the object to which the events belong is that every listener must be given a reference to the object. In situations where there are potentially many objects listening, that strategy requires too much boilerplate code to be maintainable.

Another problem you might encounter is that listeners must be tightly coupled to emitters, which partially defeats the purpose of using events in the first place. To get around that, you can wire up emitters and receivers through an event mediator or connector.

In cases where you have nested views that need to communicate up to the top level, this pattern becomes problematic because at each level, the child and parent must register with each other to relay messages. In that situation, you create a lot of code overhead, and debugging event-passing bugs can become very painful.

 If you have an object that needs to inform your application about asynchronous events such as incoming push notifications (chat notifications, new items added to collections, etc.), an event emitter might be the right solution.

Event aggregators

In contrast to event emitters, an *event aggregator* is a central object that collects events from multiple sources and delivers them to registered subscribers. This is essentially a type of publish/subscribe pattern. An aggregator eliminates the need for specialized mediators to keep an emitter and listener decoupled. Again, with Backbone and Underscore, that might look something like this:

```
// Set up an aggregator on your app object.
var app = {
  bus: _.extend({}, Backbone.Events)
};

// In your logger module, log all invites in the app.
app.bus.on('invite', function handle(inviteData) {
  console.log(inviteData);
});

// Trigger an event when a user invites a friend.
app.bus.trigger('invite', {
  user: 'userId',
```

```
    friend: 'friend.email@example.com'
});
```

Event aggregators can be enormously useful. Because neither emitter nor subscriber need know about the other, aggregators enable very loose coupling between modules. Each only needs a reference to the aggregator. In this case, the emitter and the listener only need to know about `app.bus` and the `invite` event in order to communicate.

Queues and stacks

One disadvantage of the publish/subscribe pattern is that there is no guarantee that a message will be processed once it is broadcast.

A *message queue* is a type of event mediator that records every message it hears in a queue (or stack) for later processing. That log of messages can be permanently recorded, if needed, and the queue is actively managed, so it's possible to enforce guarantees that some listener got the message.

There is often a need for separate modules or processes to collaborate in order to process input. For example, imagine that your application is a tool for photographers. It allows photographers to upload a photo, resize it, watermark it, and then send it to various social networks automatically.

When a photo is uploaded, it's added to a processing queue. Later, a pool of photo-processing workers can independently pull jobs from the message queue as they are ready to process them, and message back when the photos are ready to be distributed across the Web. Other workers can then pick up the finished photo messages and handle the distribution step. With this architecture, the processing workers can scale independently of the distribution workers.

If you need a message queue, you might be in luck. It's such a common pattern that there are several popular out-of-the-box solutions, such as Kestrel (*http://robey.github.com/kestrel/*) or Amazon Simple Queue Service (SQS) (*http://aws.amazon.com/sqs/*).

Choosing the right event model

In reality, no single event model provides a complete solution to event management. It doesn't make sense to examine a bunch of different event models and chose just one for your application. Most web-based applications eventually need more than one type. Here are some example use cases:

- For reusable libraries that deal with asynchronous behaviors, consider an event emitter.
- For communication between models, views, logging systems, analytics systems, and so on, where it's advantageous to keep coupling to a minimum, go with an event aggregator.

- For reliable communication between independently scalable and deployable application tiers, a message queue may be the right solution.

This guide has really only skimmed the surface of possible messaging patterns. I've intentionally focused only on the most common patterns that might be handy in almost every app that grows beyond a few thousand lines of code. For more ideas, take a look at Martin Fowler's writing on Event Aggregator (*http://bit.ly/1lmVSWT*), Observer Synchronization (*http://bit.ly/1lmVUxX*), and Event Sourcing (*http://bit.ly/1lmVYxD*).

Events by example

To better understand how the most common messaging patterns fit together, it might be useful to revisit the guest-list app introduced in Chapter 4.

Of course, the whole idea here is to keep the presentation concerns separate from the data-management and domain-logic concerns. Backbone.js can give you a leg up with that by encapsulating common data-management tasks in models and collections, and encapsulating display and UI concerns in views.

All `Backbone.Model` instances are event emitters. When a model attribute changes, it emits a `change:<attribute>` event, where `<attribute>` is the name of the attribute that changed. Since you want to communicate the change to the view without tightly coupling the model to the view or vice versa, you'll want to have the model listen for its own change event and rebroadcast it at the app level.

The view can listen for the app level `changed` event and respond by updating the list item that changed.

Example 5-1 shows the new guest-list model. You can listen to the `Backbone.Model` event emitter with `this.on('change:checkedIn', handler)`.

Example 5-1. guestmodel.js

```
var Model = require('backbone-browserify').Model,
  app = require('./tinyapp'),

  // Set the checkedIn attribute on the model.

  toggleCheckedIn = function toggleCheckedIn() {
    this.set('checkedIn', !this.get('checkedIn'));
  },

  delegate = function delegate() {
    var sourceId = this.get('id');

    // Listen for toggled event, sent from the view.
    // sourceId is used to filter the event. The model
    // does not need to know where the event comes from,
    // only which item was clicked.
```

```
app.on('toggled-checkedin', sourceId,
  toggleCheckedIn.bind(this));


// Relay the change event so the view can listen for it
// without knowing anything about the model.

this.on('change:checkedIn', function (item) {

  // Send a shallow copy of the list item as the
  // message payload. Make sure the new checkedIn
  // state is easy to access.

  var event = app.extend({}, item, {
    sourceId: this.id,
    checkedIn: item.get('checkedIn')
  });


  // Broadcast the message on the aggregator.

  app.trigger('changed.checkedIn', event);
}.bind(this));
},

// The collection expects a Backbone.Model constructor.

api = Model.extend({
  initialize: delegate,
  toggleCheckedIn: toggleCheckedIn
});

module.exports = api;
```

Note the line:

```
app.on('toggled-checkedin', sourceId,
  toggleCheckedIn.bind(this));
```

Tinyapp adds the concept of a sourceId to event listening. The idea is that you augment your triggered event object with the ID of the object you're talking about. When you listen for the event (like this example illustrates), you can pass in the object's ID to filter out any events that don't have that sourceId on the event object. This can be handled at the application framework or event library level. For example, in Tinyapp, there's a wrapper around the events.on method that looks something like this:

```
function on() {
  var args = [].slice.call(arguments),
    type = args[0],
    sourceId = args[1],
    callback = args[2];
```

```
    // If there's no sourceId, just pass this through
    // to the event emitter.

    if (args.length <= 2) {
      events.on.apply(events, arguments);
    } else {


      // Otherwise, filter out any events that don't match
      // the expected sourceId.

      events.on.call(events, type, function (event) {
        if (event.sourceId === sourceId) {
          callback(event);
        }
      });
    }
  }
```

Similar strategies include namespacing events and creating separate channels (aggregators) for separate concerns.

 Regardless of which mechanism you prefer for event communication, be careful not to refer to other modules directly (including via channels and namespaces). If modules know how to communicate with each other directly, it defeats the purpose of loose coupling, and you might as well give them a direct handle on each other. A common pitfall that I have fallen into myself is to use the module's namespace as the event namespace. Doing so gives every module that needs to listen knowledge of the emitting module by name.

Returning to the example app: the collection isn't doing much yet, but later you'll use it to add and remove guests. For now, it just gets a handle to the model constructor that it will use to instantiate new list items. The `create` method is just a thin wrapper around collection instantiation, as shown in Example 5-2.

Example 5-2. guestlistcollection.js

```
var app = require('./tinyapp'),
  Model = require('./guestmodel'),
  Collection = require('backbone-browserify')
    .Collection.extend({
      model: Model
    }),

  create = function create(models) {
    models = models || app.pageData.guestList;

    return new Collection(models);
  },
```

```
  api = {
    create: create
  };

module.exports = api;
```

Similar to how the model relays its own events, the view listens for DOM events and relays them on the app event aggregator so that other modules can listen (such as models or click loggers). Pay special attention to the delegate() and relayClick() functions, as in Example 5-3.

Example 5-3. guestlistview.js

```
var app = require('./tinyapp'),

  // Assign Backbone.View to the View var.

  View = require('backbone-browserify').View,

  $ = app.$,
  checkedinClass = 'icon-check',
  listClass = 'dropdown-menu',
  guestClass = 'guest',


  // Rebroadcast DOM click events on the app event
  // aggregator.

  relayClick = function relayClick(e) {

    // Get the ID from the element and use it to
    // namespace the event.

    var sourceId = $(this).attr('id'),
      event = app.extend(e, {
        sourceId: $(this).attr('id')
      });

    app.trigger('toggled-checkedin', event);
  },

  delegate = function delegate() {

    // Delegate all click events to the parent element.

    this.$el.on('click', '.' + guestClass, relayClick);

    // Listen for changed events from the model
    // and make sure the element reflects the current
    // state.
```

```
      app.on('changed.checkedIn', function changeHandler(event) {
        var id = event.id;


        // Select the right list item by ID.

        this.$el.find('#' + id)
          .toggleClass(checkedinClass, event.checkedIn);

      }.bind(this));
    },

    render = function render(guestlist) {
      var $el = this.$el;

      $el.empty();

      // Loop over the passed-in guest models and render
      // them as li elements.

      guestlist.forEach(function (guestModel) {
        var $guest;
        guest = guestModel.toJSON();
        $guest = $('<li class="' + guestClass + '" ' +
          'id="' + guest.id +'">' +
          '<span class="name">' + guest.name +
          '</span></li>');
        $guest.appendTo($el);
      });

      return this;
    },

    // Define the backbone view.
    GuestlistView = View.extend({
      tagName: 'ol',
      id: 'guestlist-view',
      className: listClass,
      initialize: delegate,
      render: render
    }),

    // Expose a factory function.
    create = function create() {
      return new GuestlistView();
    },

    api = {
      create: create
    };

module.exports = api;
```

Model View Controller/MV*

MVC (Model View Controller) is an architecture for managing separation of presentation logic from business domain logic in applications.

Model refers to application state, and methods for manipulating and retrieving state. Usually there is a mechanism to notify observing views when the model state changes. There can be more than one view listening to a single model.

View refers to the UI that gets drawn to the screen. It generally listens to the model so that it can update the UI when state changes, and sometimes to the controller so that it can handle presentation changes that do not impact the business domain (such as scrolling or showing/hiding UI).

Controller refers to the user interaction logic. It updates the model in response to user requests. In some MVC interpretations, it is responsible for instantiating both the model and the view, and wiring up event listeners between them. Most server-side web frameworks have controllers that route incoming requests to actions, which manipulate the model and serve updated views to the user. See Figure 5-1.

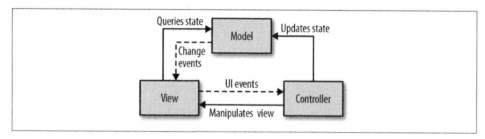

Figure 5-1. MVC

In the browser, where each element in the DOM also happens to be an event emitter with most of its own logic built in, it might seem natural to handle a bit more of the input directly in the view (rather than the controller, as is common with MVC). Several alternatives to MVC have sprung up that deviate slightly from the MVC architecture. The alternatives are commonly grouped together and referred to as *MV**. Typically, there will be a notion of a model and a view (or something like them), while many of the responsibilities of a controller will be shuffled around to other components. UI logic typically moves mostly into the view, while domain logic gets shifted largely to models. Controllers in modern web applications often get whittled down to simple routers.

For example, Angular (*https://angularjs.org/*) uses a system similar to MVC, except that the view takes on a lot of UI interaction tasks (called directives) that may have been handled by a traditional controller, and the controller handles domain logic and interactions with the models, which are bound to views via simple data structures called scopes. Angular's controllers might remind you a lot of models from other MVC implementations, if you're a follower of the "fat models, skinny controllers" approach. They typically supply or consume a collection of related services.

Riot.js (*https://muut.com/riotjs/*) is a Model View Presenter (MVP) library that represents the polar opposite of Angular. Riot's model contains only business-domain logic: state and services to manipulate that state. The view is strictly HTML and CSS. The templates contain zero logic. There are no custom extensions to the HTML. The presenter listens to both the model and the view and responds to the events. This pattern is a branch of MVP known as passive view. The approach is extraordinarily simple, and it's reflected in both the size and performance of Riot. It weighs in at less than 2 k minified and gzipped, and the template engine significantly outperforms popular competitors. The surface area of the API is so small, you could literally master it in a single sitting.

The most popular MV* library is Backbone (*http://backbonejs.org/*). As with Angular, Backbone delegates most of what you would find in a controller to the view and router. Instead of models, views, and controllers, and an opinionated way of stitching them together, Backbone defines `View`, `Model`, `Collection`, and `Router` constructors. You are expected to subclass those constructors using the `.extend()` method available on each of the constructors.

 Backbone's `.extend()` method creates classical-style inheritance hierarchies, with all the pitfalls that go along with them. I have seen a couple of projects get into trouble by relying too much on Backbone's `.extend()` inheritance. Be careful about subclassing from subclasses. Instead, try passing exemplar prototypes and mixins into `.extend()` in order to facilitate code reuse. See "Classical Inheritance Is Obsolete" on page 48 and "Prototypes" on page 53.

Backbone is not terribly opinionated about how you stitch the various pieces together, but most samples you'll find in the wild give a lot of responsibility to the view, which typically instantiates and keeps a reference to collections, models, or both. A typical arrangement might look something like Figure 5-2.

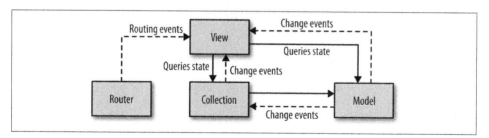

Figure 5-2. Backbone

Backbone.Router allows you to update the location bar when the user selects different views, or create actions that get triggered in response to the user navigating to a given URL. This is the primary responsibility of controllers on the server side, because URLs are generally the only way for the user to communicate with a server-side application. That's not the case in a client-side application.

Backbone.View is responsible for encapsulating view logic, such as how and when to display information. Views typically listen for DOM events, translate them into some intended action, and then emit events that the model can subscribe to.

 It's common to see views directly update models, collections, and routers, but when they do, it is a slippery slope. Often, developers get confused and start to put too much business logic in the view, which breaks the separation of concerns and leads to code duplication and hard-to-find bugs across multiple views that need to share the same business rules. Instead, views should only manage the presentation concerns and trigger events that other modules can listen for.

Backbone.Model is responsible for encapsulating state and business logic. When state changes, it emits events that views can subscribe to.

Backbone.Collection is an extremely useful abstraction that provides a managed way of dealing with collections of models, complete with Underscore's many functional methods, which you can use to query, filter, and sort your collections.

As you've already seen in the event examples, there are alternative ways to stitch Backbone's tools together. For example, you can route most of the communication through an event aggregator to reduce coupling to a minimum, as shown in Figure 5-3.

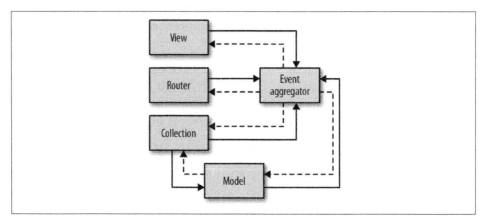

Figure 5-3. Backbone with event aggregator

The solid lines represent direct references. Dashed lines represent event listeners. As you can see, with this setup, you don't need a lot of direct references, which allows your modules to be a lot less coupled. Views listen for state changes and view selection events and emit user-action events. The router listens for user route selections, and emits route-change events. Collections listen for add and remove events and relay change events from the model. The model listens for UI input changes and emits change events.

This is the pattern you'll see developing in the examples, but it's certainly not the only way to handle separation of concerns in the browser.

There are many other MV* alternatives, including MVVM and RVP. I'll leave it to you and Google to work out how they all differ. The important thing to understand is that all of them exist to allow the separation of presentation logic and business-domain logic. In short, your business logic should not be mixed in with your presentation logic and vice versa. You can explore various libraries frameworks at TodoMVC.com (*http://todomvc.com/*).

Presentation and DOM Manipulation

The primary purpose of a view in Backbone is to present the application's interface to the user and react to user input. As such, every Backbone view should be associated with some DOM. Backbone handles that association with the `.el` and `.$el` properties. The `.el` property is a direct reference to the view's root element, while `.$el` is a cached jQuery or Zepto object for the view's element.

Consider Example 5-4 from *guestlistview.js*.

Example 5-4. Creating a Backbone view

```
// Define the backbone view.
GuestlistView = View.extend({
  tagName: 'ol',
  id: 'guestlist-view',
  className: listClass,
  initialize: delegate,
  render: render
}),
```

If specified, Backbone.View will construct `this.el` using the `tagName`, `className`, `id`, and `attributes` parameters. If you don't specify a `tagName`, it will create a `div`. You can also attach the view to an existing element by passing in a value for `.el`.

View events

Backbone lets you pass in an events hash to declaratively specify event handlers. The hash takes the form, `{ 'eventName selector': 'callback' }`. If `'callback'` is a string, it will map to the method on the view object that matches the name. You can also pass an inline function or function reference. Backbone uses jQuery's `.on()` method and delegates events to the view's root element (`this.el`) by default. If you omit the selector, the root element will be the target element.

Leaving off the selector is probably a code smell. Could you be delegating events to a parent element instead?

Event delegation. *Event delegation* is the process of aggregating events from multiple sources to a single event-handling mechanism. It's common to encounter large collections that share the same event handlers but attach different listeners for each item in the collection.

For example, it might have been tempting to implement the guest-list item as a separate view, and then rerender the guest template every time the status changed. That might look something like this:

```
render = function render(data) {
  var $el = this.$el;

  // Prevent memory leaks in rerender cases.
  $el.off('click.' + this.className);
  $el.empty();

  processTemplate($el, data);

  // Reattach listener.
  $el.on('click.' + this.className, handleClick);

  return this;
};
```

Note that this is essentially equivalent to passing an `events` hash to Backbone in the hypothetical guests `View.extend()`:

```
events: {
  'click': handleClick
}
```

Note that Backbone automatically delegates using jQuery's `.on()` method. However, passing a hash like this into an item-level view negates that capability. Instead, it will wire up a separate click handler for each list item.

This approach slows down the application in two ways: first, it takes longer to initialize because of the extra wiring that must be performed for each event handler, for each item. It also consumes more memory, particularly if you chose the inline method to specify the event handler. If you do that, there will actually be a separate copy of the event handler function for each item.

You should be aware that you can leak memory if you bind event handlers to each item in a dynamic collection. For example, if you have a collection that utilizes the infinite scroll technique, you'll need to remove elements from the DOM as they scroll out of view to prevent browser performance issues or crashes. You must remember to remove the event listeners when you remove the items from the DOM. Backbone views have a `.remove()` method that will remove both the DOM listeners and stop the view from listening for events from other objects.

You've already seen event delegation employed in the `guestlistview.js delegate()` function. Now you'll use the built in `Backbone.View` events hash to handle it instead. Here's what the delegation looked like before:

```
// From the delegate() function:
// Delegate all click events to the parent element.
this.$el.on('click', '.' + guestClass, relayClick);
```

You'll pull that code out of the delegate() function and let Backbone handle it for you:

```
// Define the backbone view.
GuestlistView = View.extend({
  tagName: 'ol',
  id: 'guestlist-view',
  className: listClass,
  initialize: delegate,
  render: render,

  // Add the handler to the view object:
  relayClick: relayClick,

  // Let Backbone handle the event delegation:
  events: {
    'click .guest': 'relayClick'
  }
}),
```

By delegating the `click` to the parent element instead of to each list item, only one listener has to be attached per behavior, rather than one per behavior for each item in the list. What's more, you don't have to worry about removing the listener and adding it again if you need to render a list item again. In short, less code to write, and less risk of memory leaks.

Bonus: when you expose your event handlers on the view object, it makes them easier to unit test because you don't have to figure out how to simulate the events in order to invoke the handlers. Keep in mind that events are a part of the API surface area, and event handlers should be tested, just like public methods.

If you implement list items as subviews, you still need to remember to call the item's `.remove()` method as the item scrolls away, because you still need to stop the view from listening to Backbone events. If you wire up any other kind of event listener (such as an app-level event aggregator), you should remember to remove those listeners as well.

Templates

Templates help to separate display structure concerns from logic. Templates define the structure of your UI, along with some indication of where data should be injected. Templates can be reused with a variety of different data. A template processor combines data and templates to produce the DOM output that will be rendered to the screen.

 It's common for template languages to support limited logic, such as if/else statements. I recommend that you avoid the temptation to use any of them, because they defeat the purpose of separating DOM structure from logic concerns—instead, your logic just lives somewhere else. Even worse, your logic lives in two places, and it's even harder to find the source of bugs.

There are many different options for template rendering. Some common choices include Jade, Mustache, Haml, EJS, Plates, and Pure. Plates (a Flatiron library) and Pure provide the ability to write templates in pure HTML, with no specialized DSL mixed in at all. Data gets associated via CSS-style selectors in the JavaScript view layer. Backbone relies on the Underscore library, which happens to include a simple template engine. For the sake of simplicity and familiarity, you'll see it used in the examples.

Let's revisit the guest-list view and replace the inline HTML with a template.

Before:

```
'<li class="' + guestClass +
  '" ' + 'id="' + guest.id +'">' +
  '<span class="name">' + guest.name +
  '</span></li>'
```

After:

```
<li class="<%= guestClass %>" id="<%= id %>">
  <span class="name"><%= name %></span>
</li>
```

Even better, now that it isn't expressed in a JavaScript string, it's obvious that it doesn't belong in the JavaScript view layer at all. For a template this small, it wouldn't do any harm to simply embed it in the HTML for the page. You can do that using a `<script>` tag:

```
<script id="guest" type="text/template">
  <li class="<%= guestClass %>" id="<%= id %>">
    <span class="name"><%= name %></span>
  </li>
</script>
```

 Unless they are tiny (a few lines), most templates should be in dedicated files. You may want to group them with corresponding views in the directory hierarchy. You can use a build step to pull templates into your HTML, or for templates that are only used rarely, fetch them as needed via Ajax.

If you're using a module system that doesn't pollute the global namespace, you'll need to explicitly require Underscore in order to access the template utility. If you're just including Backbone standalone, you don't need to do anything special to use Underscore's methods. Just use `_.template()` directly. In this case, Browserify will not leak dependencies into the global namespace, so you'll need to require it. In *guestlistview.js*, you'll insert the `require()` line like this:

```
// Assign Backbone.View to the View var.
View = require('backbone-browserify').View,

// Grab the template utility from Underscore.
template = require('underscore').template,
```

Of course, this isn't going to work until we add Underscore to *package.json*:

```
"underscore": "*",
```

Save the file and run:

```
$ npm install
```

Now that the dependency is there, it's time to add the template code. Underscore lets you compile your HTML templates into an executable function in order to speed up template processing. You can do that near the top of the `render()` function so that it doesn't need to be called for every guest that gets rendered, as in Example 5-5.

Example 5-5. render() with template

```
render = function render(guestlist) {
  var $el = this.$el,

    // Compile the guest template.
    guestTemplate = template($('#guestTemplate').html());

  $el.empty();


  // Loop over the passed-in guest models and render
  // them as li elements.
```

```
guestlist.forEach(function (guestModel) {
  var guest;

  // Build the data object to pass into the template.
  guest = guestModel.toJSON();

  // Add the guestClass to the data object.
  guest.guestClass = guestClass;

  // Process the template data and append the output to the
  // list element.
  $el.append(guestTemplate(guest));
});

  return this;
}
```

Remember to run grunt to rebuild the project files, or set up a grunt watch task to build on file save. The tests should pass again. Having the lint and unit test tasks set up makes it easy to refactor like this with confidence, because you'll catch any mistakes early.

Web Components

Web Components are a new standard way of creating reusable components and widgets with JavaScript, HTML, and CSS. The new standards currently lack widespread browser support but may soon transform the way we write reusable components for JavaScript applications.

 Shadow DOM + custom elements = Web Components.

Web Components use a technology called *Shadow DOM*, which allows you to hide an entirely new document context, including HTML, CSS, and JavaScript. Shadow DOM is completely encapsulated from the main document. It gets its own document root (called *shadow root*), and possibly in the future, its own execution context for JavaScript. Shadow DOM is also minimally affected by the CSS on the parent page. The DOM encapsulation features should feel familiar to anyone who has used iframes for encapsulation purposes.

Your shadow DOM can be made up of many other HTML elements, but they won't be visible in the DOM tree unless you specifically enable shadow DOM viewing in a debugger, such as Chrome Developer Tools.

Custom tags are an important aspect of Web Components that allow you to simplify your DOM and write more semantic HTML. For example, if you need to create a knob widget, you can create a component called <x-knob>, which reads a lot better than <div class="knob">. Custom tags can use prototypal inheritance to inherit the properties of other tags. You can simplify the creation of <x-knob> by sharing the prototype from <input> and setting some default properties (for example, by selecting type="range"). Use the new DOM method, document.register() to define the element.

Example 5-6 shows how you might define <x-knob> using the document.register() polyfill from Mozilla Web Components:

Example 5-6. document.register()

```
document.register('x-knob', {

  'prototype': Object.create( (window.HTMLInputElement ||
    window.HTMLSpanElement || window.HTMLElement).prototype ),

  'lifecycle': {

    created: function(proto) {
      this.type='range';
      console.log('x-knob created', this);
    },

    inserted: function() {
      console.log('x-knob inserted', this);
    },

    removed: function() {
      console.log('x-knob removed', this);
    },

    attributeChanged: function(attr, value) {
      console.log('x-knob attributeChanged', this, attr, value);
    }

  }
});
```

Now that you have a definition, you can instantiate it with:

```
var knob = document.createElement('x-knob');
```

Take a closer look at what happens in Example 5-7.

Example 5-7. Custom tag tests

```
$(function () {

  test('document.register()', function () {
```

```
      equal(typeof document.register, 'function',
        'Should exist.');

  });

  test('document.createElement("x-knob")', function () {
    var knob = document.createElement('x-knob');

    ok(knob.getAttribute,
      'should produce a custom element.');
  });

  test('x-knob inheritance', function () {
    var knob = document.createElement('x-knob');

    ok(knob.checkValidity,
      'should inherit from input element.');
  });

  test('x-knob input type', function () {
    var knob = document.createElement('x-knob');

    equal(knob.type, 'range',
      'should have type="range".');
  });

});
```

As exciting as all this is, it's still bleeding edge. There is currently disagreement in the community about this mechanism, arguing that if we go down this road, we'll lose a lot of the semantic meaning that the community has pushed so hard for. Ian Hickson argues along these lines:

Wouldn't it be better to add a new attribute so that we can preserve the semantics of existing elements? For example: <input is="knob" type="range">. An obvious counter argument is that popular tags will become part of the semantic vernacular, and that agents will begin to recognize them, just as they recognize the semantics of many metadata formats, and many semantic extensions built on top of vanilla HTML. Another counter argument is that many custom elements will not have meaningful base elements whose semantics would be useful to build on.

As of this writing, none of these features are available for production use if you want solid cross-browser support. Mozilla has created a custom tag polyfill (*http://github.com/mozilla/web-components*) that you can experiment with today for nonproduction use.

More recently, Google has been hard at work on Polymer (*http://www.polymer-project.org/*), which seems to be more actively maintained, more current, and more complete. Polymer Platform provides polyfills for custom elements, shadow DOM,

HTML imports, pointer events (hardware-agnostic pointer inputs for mouse, pen, and touchscreen), and web animations. Polymer Core builds an API on top of Polymer Platform polyfills, providing sugar to make it easier to work with web components. Polymer Elements is a library of reusable custom elements built on top of the Polymer Platform and Polymer Core base layers. As of this writing, Polymer is still in *alpha*, meaning that it's in an experimental state, and breaking changes might be introduced. However, it's a very promising start and could be production ready soon. Refer to the Polymer website (*http://www.polymer-project.org/*) for the current status and documentation.

Server-Side Concerns

There was a time when the server side did a lot of work, but that time has come and gone in the world of JavaScript applications. Many current JavaScript applications defer most of the rendering and business logic to the client. For most apps, the server side will look something like this:

1. RESTful or REST-like API.
2. Static file server.
3. A single-page index route that pre-injects data for the initial page load. (This can be replaced by the static file server if you defer the page data to a subsequent Ajax request.)

There are many ways to accomplish these goals, but you should have little trouble finding alternatives via Google. In this section, you'll learn how to get the job done with Node and Express.

Getting Started with Node and Express

Node is a server-side JavaScript environment with many attractive features:

- A fast JavaScript engine (built on V8).
- Asynchronous by default philosophy (nothing should block).
- Event-loop design (much like the browser environment).
- Networking as a first-class citizen (create production-capable servers with few lines of code).
- A highly usable streams API.
- A large, rapidly growing developer community.
- A simple, CommonJS-based module solution that guarantees module encapsulation (your var declarations are limited to module scope). See "Node-Style Modules" on page 82.

- A developer-friendly package management system with thousands of open-source packages to choose from.

Some of these features might take some getting used to if you are accustomed to server-side environments that allow features such as blocking IO and a single thread per connection (for convenient state management). However, you'll find that the incredible performance boost achieved by nonblocking request/response cycles is well worth the learning effort.

Don't underestimate the value of the asynchronous-by-default philosophy. That is the key to Node's incredible performance in production environments.

Where other environments force users to wait in line while files load or network operations take place, Node fires off the request and keeps accepting new connections and executing other code paths while the asynchronous event does its work in the background.

Processes can spend an incredible amount of time waiting for file reads and network requests, especially if they encounter an error. Node just keeps cruising along. It's like getting out of congested city streets with stop lights at every block and on to an open freeway.

Node isn't fast simply because of the performance of the V8 JavaScript engine (though that does help). It's fast because it doesn't waste time waiting around for things to happen. There are other platforms that share some of JavaScript's performance characteristics: Twisted Python and Tornado spring to mind. They're fast for the same reason. However, even though they are more mature, they can't compete with the active membership of the JavaScript developer community.

Node comes packaged with a module management solution called npm. It gives you access to a package registry stocked with thousands of open source packages and makes it very easy for you to contribute your own or use a private git repository for proprietary work. Of course, it's easy to mix and match open source and proprietary packages in a single application.

Installing Node and Express

First, make sure you have Node installed. There are installers available from the Node homepage (*http://nodejs.org*), but I like to use nvm so that I can easily switch between different versions of Node. To install Node with nvm:

```
$ curl https://raw.github.com/creationix/nvm/master/install.sh | sh
```

For more on nvm, check out the docs on the GitHub repository (*https://github.com/creationix/nvm*). With Node installed, you'll need to create a new directory for your project:

```
$ mkdir my-first-project
$ cd my-first project
```

Then initialize your project:

```
$ npm init
```

Express is currently the most popular application framework for Node. It's easy to learn and use, and it has a vibrant developer community. If you're going to build applications in Node, chances are you'll eventually use Express. There's no time like the present to get started. Install Express:

```
$ npm install --save express
```

That's it. You're ready to get started!

If this is your first time using Node and Express, it might be helpful to see what some of the community believes are the current set of best practices. Node Bootstrap (*https://github.com/inadarei/nodebootstrap*) aims to show new users some common practices in the Node/Express community, using Twitter Bootstrap. Among other things, there's an example of using the cluster module to manage multiple instances of the server (utilizing all available CPU cores).

Organizing files in Node

It's a good idea to follow the emerging file organization trends in existing, popular Node repositories. That way, anybody familiar with Node should be able to find their way around your repository. Here are some common file locations:

- Main *./index.js*, *./server.js*, or *./yourentryfile.js* in the root
- Supporting files in *./lib/*
- Static HTTP files in *./public/*
- Views or templates in *./views/*
- Command-line executables in *./bin/*
- Tests in *./test/* (or *./spec/* if you're a Jasmine cool-aid drinker)
- npm scripts in *./scripts/*
- Config in *./config/*
- Documentation in *./doc/*
- Examples in *./examples/*
- Performance analysis in *./benchmarks/*
- Native C/C++ source in *./source/*

The npm repository (*https://github.com/isaacs/npm*) serves as a good example.

Node libraries

These libraries will help you solve many common problems in Node:

Mout (http://moutjs.com/)
 Like Underscore/Lo-Dash, stuff that should probably be included in JavaScript

Express (http://expressjs.com/)
 Web-application framework

Q (https://github.com/kriskowal/q)
 Promises

Qconf (https://github.com/dilvie/qconf)
 Application config

Credential (https://github.com/dilvie/credential)
 Safe password hashing

Hogan (http://twitter.github.com/hogan.js/)
 Mustache for Express

Superagent (https://github.com/visionmedia/superagent)
 Communicate with APIs

Socket.io (http://socket.io/)
 Realtime communications (WebSocket)

Async (https://github.com/caolan/async)
 Asynchronous functional utilities

Bunyan (https://github.com/trentm/node-bunyan)
 Logging

Tape (https://github.com/substack/tape)
 Testing

Cuid (http://usecuid.org/)
 Better than GUID/UUID for web applications

Configuration

Don't include configuration data in your app repository (including secrets, paths to file locations, server hostnames, etc.). Instead, set up environment files with examples for sane defaults. Check in the examples, but don't check in the actual configuration. Following this rule of thumb will make deployment/ops support for the app a lot easier. Check an example file into your app repo, *s3.env.example*:

```
S3_KEY=mykey
S3_SECRET=mysecret
```

Then copy it and fill in the real values when you install the app:

```
$ cp s3.env.example s3.env
```

Use a package like qconf to make the environment variables available in your app. Make sure that the real environment files get added to `.gitignore` so that you don't accidentally check them into your repository.

 One of the first stumbling blocks you might run into moving from browsers to Node is that you can't rely on your closure state to be reserved for a single user. You have a single instance of the app, with a single pool of memory, and a potentially unbounded number of incoming connections.

State *should* be kept in a database, or passed as parameters through function calls. For example, each request in an Express application will have a corresponding request object. That may be a good place to store in-memory state for a single request/response cycle. Likewise, singletons are a good way to store state that will be shared for all requests, such as your application configuration, but otherwise, they're usually an antipattern in Node applications.

Express

There are many application frameworks available for Node. One popular framework that I find particularly useful is Express. It's basically an HTTP server built on top of Node's HTTP module and middleware.

Create your app

To create an Express app instance, you'll need to require Express and call the function that gets returned:

```
var express = require('express'),

    // Create app instance.
    app = express();
```

Routing

Express has a built-in app router. It's pretty simple to use. First, request method names correspond to the methods you call to set up your route. GET is `.get()`, POST is `.post()`, and so on. To create a route that will handle any request type, use `.all()`. Pass the route as the first parameter and a function as the second parameter:

```
app.get('/', function (req, res) {
  res.setHeader('Content-Type', 'text/plain');
```

```
    res.end('Hello, world!');
  });
```

Routes have easy parameter matching:

```
app.get('/:name', function(req, res){
  var name = req.params.name;

  res.send('Hello, ' + name);
});
```

A route can be a regular expression:

```
app.get(/(Hugh|Kevin)/, function (req, res, next) {
  var name = req.params[0], // Whitelisted user
    output;

  // Write something to output...

  res.send('Hello, ' + name);
});
```

Middleware

Middleware is software that takes an incoming request, processes it, and passes it on to the next piece of middleware in the chain. Express middleware takes the form:

```
// Add some data to the request object that your other
// middleware and routes can use.
app.use(function (req, res, next) {
  req.foo = 'bar';
  next();
});
```

Here's how it works in the context of an Express server:

```
'use strict';
var express = require('express'),

  // Create app instance.
  app = express(),

  // Use the `PORT` environment variable, or port 44444
  port = process.env.PORT || 44444;

// The new middleware adds the property `foo` to the request
// object and sets it to 'bar'.
app.use(function (req, res, next) {
  req.foo = 'bar';
  next();
});

app.get('/', function (req, res) {
  res.setHeader('Content-Type', 'text/plain');
```

```
  // Send the value passed from the middleware, above.
  res.end(req.foo);
});

app.listen(port, function () {
  console.log('Listening on port ' + port);
});
```

Point a browser at the new server, or just use curl:

```
$ curl http://localhost:44444/
bar
```

Handling errors is just as simple. Again, you'll use middleware:

```
'use strict';
var express = require('express'),

  // Create app instance.
  app = express(),

  // Use the `PORT` environment variable, or port 44444
  port = process.env.PORT || 44444;

// Some middleware that produces an error:
app.use(function (request, response, next) {
  var bar;

  try {

    // This will throw because `foo` is undefined.
    request.foo = foo.get('bar');

  } catch (error) {

    // Pass the error to the next error handler in the
    // middleware chain. If you forget `return` here,
    // it will continue to process the rest of the
    // function, and probably throw an unhandled exception.

    return next(error);
  }

  // Do something with bar.
});

// Tell express to process routes before it gets to the error handler.
app.use(app.router);


// Error handlers take four parameters. The first is the error.
// Generally, you'll want to add your error handler to the bottom of
// your app.use() stack.
```

```
app.use(function (error, request, response, next) {

  // Log the error.
  console.log(error);

  // Send the user a friendly message:
  response.send(500, 'Your request was not handled successfully. ' +
    'Our smartest fix-it guy has already been alerted. ' +
    'Contact us if you need help.');

  // Use setTimeout to give the app time to log and clean up,
  // but shut down ASAP to avoid unintended behavior.
  // Could also use setImmediate() in recent versions of Node.
  setTimeout(function () {
    process.exit(1);
  }, 0);

});

app.get('/', function (req, res) {
  res.setHeader('Content-Type', 'text/plain');

  // Sadly, nobody will ever see this friendly greeting.
  res.end('Hello, world!');
});

app.listen(port, function () {
  console.log('Listening on port ' + port);
});
```

You can clean up after a lot of errors. In fact, sometimes an error is an expected probability. For example, there's a chance that sometimes remote services won't be available, and you can recover from that condition and try again later. However, sometimes you just won't get the answer you're looking for and there's nothing you can do to recover. You don't want to keep your server running with undefined state. In the case of errors that you can't easily recover from, it's important to shut down the process as quickly as possible.

Let it crash. Processes crash. Like all things, your server's runtime will expire. Don't sweat it. Log the error, shut down the server, and launch a new instance. You can use Node's cluster module, forever (a Node module available on npm), or a wide range of other server monitor utilities to detect crashes and repair the service in order to keep things running smoothly, even in the face of unexpected exceptions.

Templates

Express comes with some built-in handling of templates, but it must be configured. You have to tell Express which view engine to use in order to process templates, and where to find the views. First, you'll want to require your template engine. For Mustache templates, you can use Hogan:

```
var hulk = require('hulk-hogan');
```

Most of the settings for Express are specified with `app.set()`. You'll need to use it to configure Express to use the template engine of your choice. There are four options that you should be aware of:

```
// Tell express where to find your templates.
app.set('views', __dirname + '/views');

// By default, Express will use a generic HTML wrapper (a layout)
// to render all your pages. If you don't need that, turn it off.
app.set('view options', {layout: false});

// Tell express which engine to use.
app.set('view engine', 'hulk-hogan');

// Specify the extension you'll use for your views.
app.engine('.html', hulk.__express);
```

Remember to define a route that uses your new view. Assuming you've used your middleware to build a data object on the request object called `req.data` (see "Middleware" on page 130):

```
app.all('/', function (req, res) {
  res.render('index', req.data, function callback(err, html) {
    // Handle error.
  });
});
```

You can leave off the callback parameter and any errors will be internally passed via `next(err)` for your generic error handlers to catch. If you pass the callback, that automatic error handling will not occur, and you should handle the error explicitly.

Next steps

Of course, you want to do a lot more with your app than return a hard-coded message to your users. The good news is that there are drivers for just about any database you can dream of. You can use a variety of template libraries, and of course, serve static files. I encourage you to dive into the Node module playground and take a look around. For starters, here's a simple static file server example using the built-in static middleware:

```
var express = require('express'),

    app = express(), // Create the express app.

    // Try pulling the port from the environment. Or
    // default to 5555 if no environment variable is set.
    port = +process.env.PORT || 5555;
```

```
// .bodyParser() parses the request body and creates the
// req.body object.
app.use( express.bodyParser() );

// .methodOverride() lets you simulate DELETE and PUT
// methods with POST methods. Common boilerplate.
app.use( express.methodOverride() );

// .static() creates a static file server, which looks for
// assets in the /public directory, in this case.
app.use( express.static(__dirname + '/public') );

// app.router handles path routing for express apps.
app.use( app.router );

// Express comes with a default error handler that is
// intended for development use. You'll want to implement
// your own for production systems.
app.use( express.errorHandler() );

app.listen(port, function () {
  console.log('Server listening on port ' + port);
});
```

Have a look at the Express guide (*http://expressjs.com/guide.html*) and API reference (*http://expressjs.com/api.html*) for a lot more useful examples, and the Node manual (*http://nodejs.org/api/*) for Node API documentation. There are lots of useful gems that you'll want to learn more about.

Conclusion

The key takeaways you should internalize from this chapter are:

- Think of your application in terms of layers of responsibility.
- Let layer separations inform your decisions about what should be included in each application tier.
- Think about the relationships between modules, layers, and tiers in your application. How will you organize them?
- Be aware when you're passing information between different layers. Which messaging patterns will be most effective for communication?
- Minimize intermodule and interlayer coupling. Use patterns like event emitters and facades to reduce the impact to dependent layers when you change something in another layer.
- Maintain separation between your domain layer (data/business logic) and your presentation layer.

You should be aware by now why it's important to separate different layers of respon-sibility into different application modules and tiers, and now that you've seen some tools and examples, you should be able to decide when and where to apply various techniques to you own applications.

The next few chapters will cover some concerns that almost every application needs to deal with at some point. For each one, try to keep in mind how the functionality being described can be implemented without intermingling user interface logic with the busi-ness domain.

## CHAPTER 6

Access Control

Access control models are responsible for granting or restricting access to resources. They depend on two things: user identification (verified by one or more authentication schemes) and feature authorization.

Before you grant access to a resource, you need to know that the user is who she claims to be (authentication) and whether or not the user should have access to a given resource (authorization).

Authentication

Authentication is the mechanism that confirms the identity of users trying to access a system. In order for users to be granted access to a resource, they must first prove that they are who they claim to be. Generally this is handled by passing a key with each request (often called an access token). The server verifies that the access token is genuine, and that the user does indeed have the required privileges to access the requested resource. Only then is the request granted.

There are many ways to grant a user an access token. The most common is a password challenge.

Passwords

Passwords should be stored with a one-way encryption hash, so that even if a malicious intruder obtains access to the user database, he still won't have access to user passwords. The hash should be long enough to prevent an attack from a single machine and to prevent an attack from a large cluster of machines. I recommend 512 bits (64 bytes).

Worms targeting vulnerable versions of popular website platforms such as WordPress and Drupal have become common. Once such worm takes control of a website and installs its payload, recruits all of the site's traffic into a JavaScript botnet, and, among other things, uses visitor CPU power to crack stolen password databases that fail to implement the security precautions outlined here.

There are botnets that exist today with over 90,000 nodes (*http://onforb.es/1pFKBSH*). Such botnets could crack MD5 password hashes at a rate of nine billion per second.

Passwords are vulnerable to the following common attacks:

- Rainbow tables
- Brute force
- Variable time equality
- Passwords stolen from third parties

Rainbow tables

Rainbow tables are precomputed tables used to look up passwords using stolen hashes. Once bad guys get their hands on user passwords, they'll attempt to attack popular services such as email and bank accounts—which spells very bad PR for your service.

There are rainbow tables that exist today (*http://bit.ly/1pFKFBT*) that can discover almost every possible password up to 14 characters. To prevent password theft by rainbow table, users should choose passwords of at least 14 characters (*http://en.wikipedia.org/wiki/Rainbow_table*). Sadly, such passwords are definitely not convenient, particularly on mobile devices. In other words, don't trust users to select appropriate passwords.

Rainbow tables can significantly reduce the time it takes to find a password, at the cost of memory, but with terabyte hard drives and gigabytes of RAM, it's a trade-off that is easily made. That said, it is possible to protect your service against rainbow table attacks.

Password salts. One defense you can employ against rainbow tables is password salting. A salt is a sequence of random characters that gets paired with a password during the hashing process. Salts should be cryptographically secure random values of a length equal to the hash size. Salts are not secrets and can be safely stored in plain text alongside the user's other credentials.

Salting can protect passwords in a couple of ways:

First, a uniquely generated salt can protect your password databases against existing rainbow tables. Using a random salt makes your site immune from these attacks. However, if you use the same salt for every password, a new rainbow table can be generated to attack the password database.

Second, if two different users utilize the same password, the compromised password will grant access to both user accounts. To prevent that, you must use a unique salt for each password. Doing so makes a rainbow table attack impractical.

Node.js supplies a suitable random generator called `crypto.randomBytes()`. It returns a buffer. Wrap it to get a suitable salt string:

```
/**
 * createSalt(keylength, callback) callback(err, salt)
 *
 * Generates a cryptographically secure random string for
 * use as a password salt using Node's built-in
 * crypto.randomBytes().
 *
 * @param   {Number} keyLength
 * @param   {Function} callback
 * @return {undefined}
 */
var createSalt = function createSalt(keyLength, callback) {
  crypto.randomBytes(keyLength, function (err, buff) {
    if (err) {
      return callback(err);
    }
    callback(null, buff.toString('base64'));
  });
};
```

The operation is asynchronous because the cryptographically secure random-number generator takes time to collect enough entropy to complete the operation.

Brute force

Rainbow tables get all the blogger attention, but Moore's law is alive and well, and brute force has become a very real threat. Attackers are employing GPUs, super-computing clusters that cost less than $2,000, and JavaScript botnets comprised of tens of thousands of browsers visiting infected websites.

A brute-force attack will attempt to crack a password by seeking a match using every possible character combination. A simple single-iteration hash can be tested at the rate of millions of hashes per second on modern systems.

One way to thwart brute-force attacks is to programatically lock a user's account after a handful of failed login attempts. However, that strategy won't protect passwords if an attacker gains access to the password database.

Key stretching can make brute-force attacks impractical by increasing the time it takes to hash the password. This can be done by applying the hash function in a loop. The delay will be relatively unnoticed by a user trying to sign in, but will significantly hamper an attacker attempting to discover a password through brute force.

Don't pick any random hash function and apply it in a loop. You could unwittingly open up attack vectors. Instead, use an established standard for iterative hashing, such as bcrypt or PBKDF2.

I discovered 100 hashes in less than 1 ms using a simple MD5 algorithm, and then tried the same thing with Node's built-in `crypto.pbkdf2()` function (HMAC-SHA1) set to 80,000 iterations. PBKDF2 took 15.48 seconds. To a user performing a single login attempt per response, the slowdown is barely noticed, but it slows brute force to a crawl.

Usage is deceptively simple:

```
crypto.pbkdf2(password, salt,
  iterations, keyLength, function (err, hash) {
    if (err) {
      return callback(err);
    }
    callback(null, new Buffer(hash).toString('base64'));
});
```

However, there are important considerations that shouldn't be overlooked, such as generating the appropriate unique, crytographically secure random salt of the right length, and calculating the number of iterations in order to balance user experience and security.

Variable time equality

If it takes your service longer to say no to a slightly wrong password than a mostly wrong password, attackers can use that data to guess the password, similar to how you guess a word-playing hangman. You might think that random time delays and network timing jitter would sufficiently mask those timing differences, but it turns out an attacker just needs to take more timing samples to filter out the noise and obtain statistically relevant timing data:

From Crosby et al. "Opportunities And Limits Of Remote Timing Attacks" (*http://www.cs.rice.edu/~dwallach/pub/crosby-timing2009.pdf*):

> We have shown that, even though the Internet induces significant timing jitter, we can reliably distinguish remote timing differences as low as 20 μs. A LAN environment has lower timing jitter, allowing us to reliably distinguish remote timing differences as small as 100 ns (possibly even smaller). These precise timing differences can be distinguished with only hundreds or possibly thousands of measurements.

The best way to beat these attacks is to use a constant time hash equality check, rather than an optimized check. That is easily achieved by iterating through the full hash before returning the answer, regardless of how soon the answer is known.

For more information, see Coda Hale's "A Lesson in Timing Attacks" (*http://codahale.com/a-lesson-in-timing-attacks/*).

Here is an example of a constant time string equality algorithm in JavaScript:

```
/**
 * constantEquals(x, y)
 *
 * Compare two strings, x and y with a constant time
 * algorithm to prevent attacks based on timing statistics.
```

```
*/
constantEquals = function constantEquals(x, y) {
  var result = true,
    length = (x.length > y.length) ? x.length : y.length,
    i;

  for (i=0; i<length; i++) {
    if (x.charCodeAt(i) !== y.charCodeAt(i)) {
      result = false;
    }
  }
  return result;
};
```

Stolen passwords

By far the biggest threat to password security is the fact that these tactics have already worked against other websites, and users have a tendency to reuse passwords across different sites. Since you don't have access to the user's other accounts for verification, there's little you can do to enforce unique passwords on your website.

As you have seen, passwords alone are an ineffective authentication system, but they can still be useful in combination with other authentication factors.

Credential

I searched for a suitable open source password authentication module in npm, but I couldn't find one that met all of the criteria you should consider when you're implementing password authentication in your applications. This is a critical component of your system security, so it's important to get it right. I created a library to make it easy.

 Credential was reviewed by a small army of security and JavaScript experts before publishing. Unless you're a security expert with access to a whole lot of other security experts, it's generally a really bad idea to roll your own security library. It's a much better idea to use something that's already well established and well tested.

Install credential:

```
$ npm install --save credential
```

.hash():

```
var pw = require('credential'),
  newPassword = 'I have a really great password.';

pw.hash(newPassword, function (err, hash) {
  if (err) { throw err; }
```

```
      console.log('Store the password hash.', hash);
    });
```

.verify():

```
    var pw = require('credential'),
      storedHash = '{"hash":...', // truncated to fit on page
      userInput = 'I have a really great password.';

    pw.verify(storedHash, userInput, function (err, isValid) {
      var msg;
      if (err) { throw err; }
      msg = isValid ? 'Passwords match!' : 'Wrong password.';
      console.log(msg);
    });
```

You can wrap this to supply a simple verify() function that takes a username and password, and then calls a callback:

```
    var users = require('./users.js');

    var verify = function verify(username, password, verified) {
      var user = users.findOne(username);
      if (!user) {
        // No unexpected error, no user, reason for failure
        return verified(null, false, {
          message: 'User not found'
        });
      }

      pw.verify(user.hash, password, function (isValid) {
        if (!isValid) {
          // No unexpected error, no user, reason for failure
          return verified(null, false, {
            message: 'Incorrect password.'
          });
        }
        return verified(null, user);
      });
    };
```

You can then plug that into something like passport-local:

```
    var express = require('express'),
      passport = require('passport'),
      LocalStrategy = require('passport-local'),
      verify = require('./lib/password-auth.js'),
      app = express();

    passport.use( new LocalStrategy(verify) );

    app.post('/login',
      passport.authenticate('local', { failureRedirect: '/login' }),
      function(req, res) {
```

```
    res.redirect('/');
  });

  app.listen(3000);
```

Multifactor Authentication

Because of the threat of stolen passwords, any policy that relies solely on password protection is unsafe. In order to protect your system from intruders, another line of defense is necessary.

Multifactor authentication is an authentication strategy that requires the user to present authentication proof from two or more authentication factors: the knowledge factor (something the user knows, like a password); the possession factor (something the user has, like a mobile phone); and the inherence factor (something the user is, like a fingerprint).

Knowledge factor

A common secondary security mechanism that was widely implemented in the financial industry just a few years ago are "security questions." Pairing a password with security questions does not qualify as multifactor authentication, though, because you need the user to pass challenges from two or more authentication factors. Using multiple knowledge factor challenges does not prevent a determined snoop from breaking in.

Multifactor authentication means that an attacker would have to be both a snoop and a thief, for instance.

Possession factor

For corporate and government intranets, it's common to require some type of physical token or key to grant access to systems. Mechanisms include USB dongles and flash card keys.

OTPs (one-time passwords) are short-lived passwords that work only for a single use. They satisfy the possession factor because they're usually generated by a dedicated piece of hardware, or by an app on the user's mobile phone. The device is paired with the service that is being authenticated against in a way that cannot be easily spoofed by impostors.

Google released a product called Google Authenticator that generates one time passwords for mobile devices. There is a node module called speakeasy that lets you take advantage of Google authenticator to authenticate users using the possession factor.

Install Speakeasy:

```
$ npm install --save speakeasy
```

Then take it for a spin:

```
var speakeasy = require('speakeasy');

// Returns a key object with ascii, hex, base32, and
// QR code representations (the QR code value is a
// Google image URL):
var key = speakeasy.generate_key({
  length: 20,
  google_auth_qr: true
});

// This should match the number on your phone:
speakeasy.time({key: key.base32, encoding: 'base32'});
```

Authy is a product similar to Google Authenticator that recently announced support for Bluetooth pairing. If your phone is near your computer, the Authy desktop agent will detect your phone's key over Bluetooth so that you won't have to type the token manually.

Inherence factor

The inherence factor is something the user is—in other words, some information that discloses some physical property of the user. Common examples include fingerprint and retina scanners. While technology does exist to scan fingerprints, retinas, palm prints, and more, it's possible to defeat security devices such as fingerprint scanners if an attacker can convince the scanner that a printed image is actually the user's fingerprint. Printed images have been used to defeat facial recognition and fingerprint scanners in cell phone devices.

Because of the risk of compromise and a user's inability to change her own fingerprints, security experts like to say that the inherence factor is equivalent to a username, not a password. In other words, inherence can be used to make user recognition more convenient but should not be used to prove the user's identity.

The closest I have seen to a security-enhancing inherence factor is a process known as geofencing. Geofencing allows you to use location APIs to determine what part of the world the current user is in. Because users travel, geofencing should be used as a warning mechanism. For example, it could be used to trigger an additional authentication using another factor. It's also worth mentioning that geofencing can be defeated by a simple web-proxy mechanism. It may discourage a casual or unsophisticated attacker, but a determined attacker may eventually defeat it.

You can use the new HTML Geolocation API to establish compliance the location of the user, provided that the user grants permission. The following function will return the user's geolocation in latitude and longitude:

```
var getLocation = function getLocation(cb) {
  if (!navigator.geolocation) {
    return cb(new Error('Geolocation is not supported by this browser.'));
  }
```

```
navigator.geolocation.getCurrentPosition(function (position) {
    cb(null, position);
  });
};

getLocation(function (err, position) {
  if (err) {
    return console.log(err);
  }
  console.log(position);
});
```

To use the data for geofencing, simply save users' preferred locations along with their profile, and ask them to authorize any new locations that they log in from. The size of the geofence perimeter should depend on your particular security needs. For example, a bank may chose a 5-mile radius, whereas a discussion forum may select a 50-mile radius.

Federated and Delegated Authentication

Federated authentication is a mechanism that allows users to share their identity across multiple services with a single-sign-on (SSO) solution. OpenID is a good example of a federated SSO solution, but it hasn't been widely adopted by users due to usability concerns. That could change soon with OpenID Connect, an identity solution built on top of OAuth 2.0 (similar to Facebook Connect).

Mozilla Persona

Mozilla's Persona (*http://www.mozilla.org/en-US/persona/*) is an open source federated identity system that uses email addresses and short-lived tokens for identification. Persona allows you to add login and logout buttons to your website, and watch() for login and logout actions. Persona has identity provider bridge support for both Yahoo! and Gmail. Sadly, Persona has failed to catch fire, and Mozilla announced in March 2014 that it would no longer actively develop the service.

WebID

WebID is a W3C-backed federated identity system that works in all current browsers built on top of existing web standards. Unfortunately, it currently relies on certificate selection UIs that are built into browsers—parts of the browser user interface that have long been neglected and are rather ugly and cumbersome for users. Several years after the first WebID specification was published, the UIs have not improved much.

The primary advantages of WebID are that it works over TLS and does not rely on email to prove identity. That said, no website can afford to rely on an authentication mechanism that is unfriendly to its user community.

For this reason, I can't recommend WebID for production use today, and neither does the W3C. At the time of this writing, it has not yet evolved into an official working group, and it is probably years from reaching an official recommendation state, if that ever happens.

Delegated authentication

Delegated authentication allows you to delegate authentication to a specific third-party provider (such as Facebook or Twitter). Unlike federated authentication, delegated authentication systems are not distributed, meaning that there is a single, centralized provider for identity. Your site can implement multiple delegate providers, of course. For example, you can give your users the choice to log in with Twitter or Facebook, but from the perspective of end users, they're presented with a choice of providers, and they are forced to remember which one they use to log in to your site (unless you detect that the accounts belong to the same user and link the accounts).

A single federated login mechanism tends to present a better user experience than offering users a choice of mechanisms because the user doesn't have to remember which mechanism they chose. For example, if your site implements Persona, all the user has to remember is his email address.

Facebook login is the most successful delegated authentication system as of this writing, by virtue of the size of its user base. It has a huge market saturation, and most users will be familiar with both the branding and the Facebook login and authorization flow.

To enable Facebook login on your site, first, create a new Facebook app, and then retrieve the app ID and app secret. To create a Facebook app, visit the Facebook Apps page (*https://developers.facebook.com/apps*).

Facebook supplies a JavaScript SDK to help you interact with their API. Here's the code you need to work with it:

```
<div id="fb-root"></div>
<script>
  window.fbAsyncInit = function() {
    FB.init({
      appId      : 'YOUR_APP_ID', // App ID

      // Channel File
      channelUrl : '//WWW.YOUR_DOMAIN.COM/channel.html',
      status     : true, // check login status
      // enable cookies to allow the server to access
      // the session
      cookie     : true,
      xfbml      : true  // parse XFBML
    });

    // Additional init code here
```

```
  };

  // Load the SDK asynchronously
  (function(d){
    var js,
      id = 'facebook-jssdk',
      ref = d.getElementsByTagName('script')[0];

    if (d.getElementById(id)) {return;}
    js = d.createElement('script');
    js.id = id;
    js.async = true;
    js.src = "//connect.facebook.net/en_US/all.js";
    ref.parentNode.insertBefore(js, ref);
  }(document));
</script>
```

The channel file is a single-line file that addresses cross-domain issues in some browsers. It only needs to be one line:

```
<script src="//connect.facebook.net/en_US/all.js"></script>
```

The Facebook API is notorious for changing. Visit Facebook's "Getting Started With Facebook Login" webpage (*http://bit.ly/1pFLFWv*) for the latest details.

Authorization

Authorization ensures that agents (users or applications) have access to only the resources they are allowed to access according to some attributes of the agent; resource policies, such as ACLs (access control lists); or both, as in MAC (mandatory access control) models.

An ACL is essentially a table that lists each user with access to a particular resource. ACLs can be stored at the system level, listing each user and what she can do or see within the system, or they can be stored at the resource level.

In a MAC system, each resource has an associated minimum trust level, and each user has an associated trust level. If the user is not trusted enough, access to the resource is denied.

Role-based access controls (RBAC) allow you to authorize users with specific roles. A user can have any number of roles, and a user is granted privileges based on her role. For example, a blog might have a small number of administrators who can change anything, a larger set of editors who can edit and publish posts, an even larger number of contributors who can contribute blog posts, and an open membership whereby anybody can register to post comments.

It is possible to implement MAC using role-based access controls, and it is also possible to combine the use of RBAC and ACLs.

Protecting express resources with an authorization strategy is easy:

```
app.put('/posts/:id', authorize(), putPost);
```

The `authorize()` function returns a middleware function that can check to see whether or not the user has permission to access the requested resource before the route handler has the chance to run. For example, if you want to ensure that the user is logged in, you can use an authorize function that looks like this:

```
var authorize = function authorize(options) {
  return function auth(req, res, next) {
    if (options.requiresAuth &&
        !(req.session && req.session.user)) {
      return res.send(403);
    }
    next();
  };
};
```

Authorizing Applications

Applications can act as user agents in order to access a user's data from a third-party system or even perform actions on the user's behalf, such as sharing on social networks or posting content. In order for an app to be granted such access, it must first prove that the user has authorized it. Typically that is accomplished by sending a token along with the request.

Applications gain the token using an application authorization grant. The user is directed to the target application and presented with an authorization request. If the user grants the requested permissions, a token is set and delivered to the requesting application.

Facebook's authorization is tied to the authentication system (Facebook Login). When a user attempts to log in to your app for the first time with Facebook, he will be presented with an authorization screen which displays the permissions your app asked for (called `scope`).

Facebook recommends that you ask for as few permissions as possible upfront. Requesting more than four permissions severely impedes the success rate of the authorization grant. Ask for as few as possible for your app to function properly, and then request additional permissions on an as-needed basis.

For example, initially you may only want to request access to the user's email and likes. Later on, let user actions trigger permission requests. That way, the user has context and knowledge of why you need that particular permission. Say the user wants to share a photo from your app on her own timeline. You'll want to check to see if you have been granted that permission, and if you haven't yet, ask for the `publish_actions` permission in response to her request.

The user is much more likely to grant permission if you need it to complete an action that she directly requested.

This principle holds true whether you're dealing with Facebook or any other third-party authorization.

OAuth 2.0

OAuth 2.0 is an open standard for application authorization that allows clients to access resources on behalf of the resource owner. Essentially, it allows you to grant applications limited access to your accounts on third-party services. For example, Facebook, Google Docs, and Dropbox all allow you to access resources on behalf of their users via their OAuth 2.0 based public APIs.

By way of contrast, OpenID provides a means to request the user's identity from a federated ID provider (such as Google). That identity includes details such as the user's name and email address. Google returns proof to the application that the user is who he says he is (the owner of the identity in question).

OAuth 2.0, on the other hand, returns a token that grants the app access to a specific set of API resources. Think of it this way: using an authentication system like OpenID is similar to showing your driver's license or passport. Using OAuth 2.0 is like giving the app a temporary key that it can use to access your resources on another site (but only those resources you have explicitly authorized).

OAuth 2.0 is a framework that exposes several authorization grant flows. There are specific flows for desktop apps, web apps, native mobile apps, and other devices.

A basic OAuth 2.0 flow goes something like this:

1. Client requests permissions from the user.
2. The user is directed to the third-party service that provides those permissions, where the user is authenticated and the request is granted or rejected.
3. The grant is passed back to the requesting client.
4. The client exchanges the grant for an access token.
5. In subsequent calls, the client provides the access token in order to prove that she has permission to access the requested resources.
6. Optionally, the service can implement a token exchange, whereby a client can exchange an expiring token for a fresh token.

If you'd like your app to be an OAuth 2.0 provider, check out oauth2orize (*https://github.com/jaredhanson/oauth2orize*).

To verify issued bearer tokens, you'll also need a strategy to authenticate bearer tokens. Take a look at passport-http-bearer (*https://github.com/jaredhanson/passport-http-bearer*).

OAuth 2.0 has been the subject of a lot of security criticism. Security experts cite the large attack surface and the difficulty of correct implementation as reasons to avoid using the specification as-is. However, Facebook and other providers offer bounties for users who are able to uncover security vulnerabilities in their implementations, and those bounties have led to vulnerability discoveries and patches.

Despite security concerns, OAuth 2.0 is currently the dominant form of third-party API authorization. It has the best tooling and community support.

Conclusion

Security is an essential component of your application, and it's very important to get it right. Here are some keys to remember:

- Use a good authentication library, such as Credential.
- Passwords alone are never secure. Allow multifactor authentication for your app.
- HTTP uses plain-text communication. In order to protect user passwords and data, enable HTTPS site-wide.
- As a general rule, it's a good idea to use an `authorize()` middleware for all of your routes.
- Enable OAuth 2.0 support to discourage third-party application vendors from requesting your user's login credentials.

## CHAPTER 7

Logging

Logging is a critical piece of application infrastructure, particularly in a modern Java-Script application. A typical JavaScript application will involve events in a browser, events on the server, events related to third-party API communication, and a real need for deep profiling and analysis of application performance characteristics. Logging serves every aspect of the application business, including:

- Debugging
- Server operations
- Security/intrusion detection
- Auditing
- Business analytics
- Marketing

Debugging

For debugging, it's critical to log all application errors and warnings. The log messages that serve other functions will also come in handy while you're debugging, because they can supply context when something goes wrong.

During development, it's often useful to log debug messages to investigate specific issues. In those scenarios, it's useful to log:

- The value of a related variable
- If a particular function was called
- The return value for a function call

- API responses

- The sequence of particular events

Sometimes it's useful to know which functions called which at a particular spot in your codebase. It's possible to log a stack trace with `console.trace()`:

```
var foo = function foo() {
    console.trace();
  },
  bar = function bar() {
    foo();
  };

bar();

/*
Trace
    at foo (repl:2:9)
    at bar (repl:5:1)
    at repl:1:1
    at REPLServer.self.eval (repl.js:110:21)
    at repl.js:249:20
    at REPLServer.self.eval (repl.js:122:7)
    at Interface.<anonymous> (repl.js:239:12)
    at Interface.EventEmitter.emit (events.js:95:17)
    at Interface._onLine (readline.js:202:10)
    at Interface._line (readline.js:531:8)
*/
```

It can also be useful to know the time it takes to complete a particular operation, especially if you want to avoid blocking the event loop. To find out, you can log start and end times. This is useful both for debugging purposes and for app performance profiling, to discover bottlenecks in your code:

```
console.time('timer label');

var foo = [];

// Warning: Avoid large set iterations blocking
// the event loop like this one does.
for (var i = 0, end = 1000000; i < end; i++) {
  foo[foo.length] = i;
}

console.timeEnd('timer label');

timer label: 87ms
```

The timer label names your timer so that you can refer back to it when you call `console.timeEnd()`.

Server Operations

Logs are useful for server operations. In case of a failure, it's often possible to determine which services are affected and which servers might be the source of a problem by examining the logs.

It's usually good idea to collect all of your logs in one data aggregation service so that it's easy check each critical piece of system infrastructure and ensure that it's behaving as expected. For example, you may notice that your database service is returning a higher number of errors than expected, and that could give you a great place to start looking for the source of the problem.

Security

Security breaches can be traced by examining the logs to track breakins, including originating user accounts and IP addresses. Security experts can use logs to establish a trail of breadcrumbs that can lead back to the source of the intrusion, uncover the attack vectors, and discover backdoors and malware that may have been injected.

Security forensics involves examining:

- Who was involved
- What was compromised
- When it was compromised
- How it was compromised
- Which systems were involved
- Attack vectors (intruder path and sequence of events)

Because a system that has been breached can no longer be trusted, it's important to get an offline snapshot of the system as soon as the breach is detected before attempting to perform any diagnostic operations.

Taking the system offline is similar to a police investigation taping off a crime scene. The idea is to preserve the evidence as much as possible. If the system is still active, the intruder could still be active on it, destroying evidence. Even if the intruder is long gone, the actions of the investigators could destroy evidence, like police offers covering a perpetrator's footprints with their own.

Note that with virtual machines, it's possible to take snapshots of a running machine. You can take an offline snapshot and isolate the running instance from other network components in order to lure the intruder into returning to the crime scene. As soon as the isolated system is accessed again, you've caught your perpetrator red-handed.

Using this technique, it's possible for investigators to observe the intruder's behavior in realtime in a safe, sandboxed environment. It's even possible to simulate full machine clusters with phony data.

Sandboxed clusters like this are sometimes established as a preventive measure prior to any known intrusion. The only purpose they serve is to lure intruders, so you know that any IP address that accesses the system is suspect. Cross-checking those IP addresses with the access logs of your other machines can reveal intrusion vectors that might otherwise go unnoticed.

Auditing

Some organizations require in-depth audit trails of every user of the system in order to verify policy compliance. In those cases, any time a user is authenticated or authorized, that event should be logged for auditing purposes. Every authentication or authorization attempt should be logged, regardless of the outcome. Combined with the detailed logs collected for security purposes and general analytics, you should be able to piece together a very detailed account of every system interaction.

Business Analytics

For business analytics, you should be logging anything that can move the needle on your business KPIs (Key Performance Indicators).

For a SaaS business (Software as a Service), there are a handful of KPIs that you must be able to measure. Be sure that you're logging enough data to calculate all of them:

Viral factor (K-factor)

Churn rate
> Percentage of users who stop using the product from one month to the next.

Monthly Recurring Revenue (MRR)
> The amount of revenue earned per customer per month.

Customer acquisition cost
> In order to calculate this value, it's important to link conversions back to campaign spending wherever possible. Be sure that marketing campaign identifiers are logged with your transactions.

Customer Lifetime Value (CLTV)
> How much does each customer spend during the lifetime of his activity, on average?

Viral Factor

Word of mouth will make or break your app. If people aren't sharing it, you won't achieve organic growth and your app will fail. The standard measure for viral factor is taken from biology's K-factor, which is designed to measure the infection potential of a virus. In order to measure it, you need to track two variables:

$i = distribution$
> Number of invites sent by existing customers before they go inactive

$c = infection$
> Invite conversion rate

With those measurements tracked, calculating k is easy:

$$k = i \times c$$

If k = 1, your application audience will remain constant. It won't grow or shrink. For k > 1, your application is in exponential growth (this is what you want).

For k < 1, your application is in exponential decline (this is the worst-case scenario).

If your app lacks an invite mechanism and a way to log invitations, you can't directly track or log distribution.

If you're not tracking conversions (new user signups), you can't calculate your application's virality. That's like flying an airplane without knowing how high above the ground you are.

Would you board an airplane with no windshield and no altitude measurement? Always track your viral factor.

Logging Checklist

Now that you have a basic overview of typical data capture needs, it might be useful to get specific about exactly what you should be logging, and how. The following checklist will help you determine what particular data you should consider logging and go into some detail about how you might log it:

- Requests from clients (GET, POST, etc.)
- Errors
- Failure alerts
- Conversion goals (sales, social-media shares, etc.)
- Authorizations (user requesting a protected resource)
- Feature activations (moving between pages and views, etc.)

- Performance metrics
- Server response time
- Time to page-ready event
- Time to page-rendered event

Logging Requests

This probably goes without saying, but for most applications, you should log all your server requests, regardless of the outcome.

For each request, you may want to log the following:

- Timestamp
- Hostname of the server (diagnose a clustered server)
- Request ID (to link related log messages together)
- Requester IP address
- Request method
- Request URL
- Request headers
- Request protocol (usually HTTP or HTTPS)
- Referrer
- User-Agent HTTP request header
- Response
- Status
- Headers
- Response time
- Request ID

What *not* to log:

- Passwords
- Secret tokens
- Credit card numbers
- Information that would hurt user privacy
- Classified information

Make sure your request serializer is set up to redact information that could compromise your users' privacy or your system security.

Your request logger should be the among the first items in your middleware stack. Something like Bunyan might come in handy. Bunyan is a lightweight logger that supports extensible streams and custom serialization of different types of log messages.

Bunyan allows you to create custom object serializers. Basically, a Bunyan serializer transforms the object you pass in to log the properties you want to log and ignore the properties you don't want to log.

You can add as many serializers as you want. It comes with serializers for req, res, and err out of the box, but you'll probably want to customize them based on the needs of your app. Here are some replacement serializers that add requestId and response Time to the standard serializers and make sure that the correct IP gets logged, even if your server is behind a reverse proxy (a very common production configuration):

```
var serializers = {
  req: function reqSerializer(req) {
    if (!req || !req.connection) {
      return req;
    }

    return {
      url: req.url,
      method: req.method,
      protocol: req.protocol,
      requestId: req.requestId,

      // In case there's a proxy server:
      ip: req.headers['x-forwarded-for'] ||
        req.connection.remoteAddress,
      headers: req.headers
    };
  },
  res: function resSerializer(res) {
    if (!res) {
      return res;
    }

    return {
      statusCode: res.statusCode,
      headers: res._header,
      requestId: res.requestId,
      responseTime: res.responseTime
    };
  },
  err: function errSerializer(err) {
    if (!err || !err.stack) {
      return err;
    }
```

```
        return {
            message: err.message,
            name: err.name,
            stack: getFullStack(err),
            code: err.code,
            signal: err.signal,
            requestId: err.requestId
        };
    }
};
```

To use a serializer, you need to pass an object with a key sharing the name of the serializer into the log call. For example, instead of:

```
log.info(req);
```

You want to trigger the request serializer by passing in the request on the req key:

```
log.info({req: req});
```

You'll want middleware to log requests, responses, and errors:

```
log.requestLogger = function
    createRequestLogger() {

  return function requestLogger(req, res,
      next) {

    // Used to calculate response times:
    var startTime = Date.now();

    // Add a unique identifier to the request.
    req.requestId = cuid();

    // Log the request
    log.info({req: req});

    // Make sure responses get logged, too:
    req.on('end', function () {
      res.responseTime = Date.now() - startTime;
      res.requestId = req.requestId;
      log.info({res: res});
    });

    next();
  };
};

log.errorLogger = function
    createErrorLogger() {

  return function errorLogger(err, req, res,
      next) {
```

```
    // Add the requestId so we can link the
    // error back to the originating request.
    err.requestId = req.requestId;

    log.error({err: err});
    next(err);
  };
};
```

Most apps will also need a way to log client-side events. For this, you can use a */log.gif* endpoint.

Counterintuitively, a GET endpoint has significant advantages over a POST endpoint for this purpose. Unlike POST requests, it can easily track email opens, goal-page views on third-party ecommerce and affiliate pages, and other events and impressions on third-party sites. For fast and flexible client-side logging, a tracking pixel is still the way to go:

```
// Tracking pixel / web bug
//
// Using a 1x1 transparent gif allows you to
// use the logger in emails or embed the
// tracking pixel on third party sites without
// requiring JavaScript.
log.route = function route() {
  return function pixel(req, res) {
    var data;

    if (settings.logParams && req.params) {
      data = mixIn({}, req.params, {
        requestId: req.requestId
      });
      log.info(req.params);
    }

    res.header('content-type', 'image/gif');

    // GIF images can be so small, it's
    // easy to just inline it instead of
    // loading from a file:
    res.send(
      'GIF89a\u0001\u0000\u0001\u0000' +
      '\u00A1\u0001\u0000\u0000\u0000\u0000' +
      '\u00FF\u00FF\u00FF\u00FF\u00FF\u00FF' +
      '\u00FF\u00FF\u00FF\u0021\u00F9\u0004' +
      '\u0001\u000A\u0000\u0001\u0000\u002C' +
      '\u0000\u0000\u0000\u0000\u0001\u0000' +
      '\u0001\u0000\u0000\u0002\u0002\u004C' +
      '\u0001\u0000;');
  };
};
```

For your convenience, I've published all this on npm as bunyan-request-logger. To use it in your app:

```
$ npm install --save bunyan-request-logger
```

There's a demo client side */log.gif* endpoint service included that shows how to use it. You can find it in *./examples/log-only.js*. Here's what it looks like:

```
'use strict';

var express = require('express'),
  logger = require('../request-logger.js'),
  noCache = require('connect-cache-control'),
  log = logger(),
  app = express(),
  port = 3000;

app.use( log.requestLogger() );

// Route to handle client side log messages.
//
// This route prepends the cache-control
// middleware so that the browser always logs
// to the server instead of fetching a useless
// OK message from its cache.
app.get( '/log.gif', noCache, log.route() );

app.listen(port, function () {
  log.info('Listening on port ' + port);
});
```

Logging Errors

In an error log message, there are three critical pieces of information:

- Timestamp
- Error message
- Stack trace

The most useful of these, perhaps, is the stack trace. It tells you where an error was thrown, right down to the line number.

In some cases, that information alone is enough to determine the root cause of the error. In other cases, you'll need to do more digging, but at least you'll know where to start looking.

To add error logging to the previous example app, from bunyan-request-logger (available in the *examples* folder):

```
// Log request errors:
app.use(log.errorLogger);
```

That refers to the following Express error handler:

```
log.errorLogger = function
    createErrorLogger() {

  return function errorLogger(err, req, res,
      next) {

    // Add the requestId so we can link the
    // error back to the originating request.
    err.requestId = req.requestId;

    log.error({err: err});
    next(err);
  };
};
```

As you can see, the middleware logs the error and passes the error to the next error handler in the middleware stack. It's easier to log first than it is to remember to add logging calls to every possible path in the error handler.

Remember, regardless of the outcome of the error handling, you're going to log the client response anyway. That's already handled by the request logger, so you don't have to worry about it.

Here's a sample app that demonstrates error logging in context. To use it, you'll need to install express-error-handler:

```
$ npm install --save express-error-handler
```

The code for the sample app is in *bunyan-request-logger/examples/app.js*:

```
'use strict';

var express = require('express'),
  logger = require('../request-logger.js'),
  noCache = require('connect-cache-control'),
  errorHandler = require('express-error-handler'),
  log = logger(),
  app = express(),
  env = process.env,
  port = env.myapp_port || 3000,
  http = require('http'),
  server;

app.use( log.requestLogger() );

// Route to handle client-side log messages.
//
// This route prepends the cache-control
```

```
// middleware so that the browser always logs
// to the server instead of fetching a useless
// OK message from its cache.
app.get( '/log.gif', noCache, log.route() );

// Route that triggers a sample error:
app.get('/error', function createError(req,
    res, next) {
  var err = new Error('Sample error');
  err.status = 500;
  next(err);
});

// Log request errors:
app.use( log.errorLogger() );

// Create the server object that we can pass
// in to the error handler:
server = http.createServer(app);

// Respond to errors and conditionally shut
// down the server. Pass in the server object
// so the error handler can shut it down
// gracefully:
app.use( errorHandler({server: server}) );

server.listen(port, function () {
  log.info('Listening on port ' + port);
});
```

Sample Log Output

Take a look at what happens in the console when you start the sample app:

```
$ cd ./node_modules/bunyan-request-logger
$ node ./examples/app.js
```

Default Bunyan log messages look like this:

```
{
    "name":"unnamed app",
    "hostname":"unnamed-host",
    "pid":62136,
    "level":30,
    "msg":"Listening on port 3000",
    "time":"2013-10-07T07:52:59.236Z",
    "v":0
}
```

The app name and host name make it easy to identify the particular source of the log message, even after it's aggregated on a different server. Anything you pass to the `log.info()` call will appear as the message, and of course, the timestamp tells you when the event was logged.

A successful GET request log entry looks like this:

```
$ curl localhost:3000/log?somedata=yay

{
    "name":"unnamed app",
    "hostname":"unnamed-host",
    "pid":62136,
    "level":30,
    "req":{
        "url":"/log?somedata=yay",
        "method":"GET",
        "protocol":"http",
        "requestId":"chmhekaby0000y0ixelvt7y7u",
        "ip":"127.0.0.1",
        "headers":{
            "user-agent":"curl/7.24.0
            (x86_64-apple-darwin12.0)
            libcurl/7.24.0 OpenSSL/0.9.8x
            zlib/1.2.5",
            "host":"localhost:3000",
            "accept":"*/*"
        }
    },
    "msg":"",
    "time":"2013-10-07T07:53:07.150Z",
    "v":0
}
```

As with the previous message, all the basics are there, but this one includes the serialized request object, including the requested URL, method, protocol, the request ID that will help you tie this log entry to other events triggered by this particular request, the user's IP address, and request headers.

The corresponding response log entry looks like this:

```
{
    "name":"unnamed app",
    "hostname":"unnamed-host",
    "pid":62136,
    "level":30,
    "res":{
        "statusCode":200,
        "headers":"HTTP/1.1 200 OK
        X-Powered-By: Express
        Expires: 0
        Cache-Control: no-store, no-cache,
        must-revalidate, max-age=0
        Pragma: no-cache
        Content-Type: text/plain
```

```
        Content-Length: 2
        Date: Mon, 07 Oct 2013 07:53:07 GMT
        Connection: keep-alive",
        "requestId":"chmhekaby0000y0ixelvt7y7u",
        "responseTime":3
    },
    "msg":"",
    "time":"2013-10-07T07:53:07.154Z",
    "v":0
}
```

This time we get the corresponding response object, including the response headers, and critically, the status code. Status codes can let you know about all sorts of problems, such as authorization issues, broken links, 500 errors, and a whole lot more. Each endpoint might have a list of expected status codes, and any log items that deviate from that list should be investigated. Again, the request ID helps you link this particular log entry to the specific request that triggered it.

When a request triggers an error, first it logs the request as usual. As you can see, there's nothing in particular about this request that would indicate that anything went wrong (yet):

```
$ curl localhost:3000/error

{
    "name":"unnamed app",
    "hostname":"unnamed-host",
    "pid":62136,
    "level":30,
    "req":{
        "url":"/error",
        "method":"GET",
        "protocol":"http",
        "requestId":"chmhekbuq0001y0ix6k6brxq6",
        "ip":"127.0.0.1",
        "headers":{
            "user-agent":"curl/7.24.0
            (x86_64-apple-darwin12.0)
            libcurl/7.24.0 OpenSSL/0.9.8x
            zlib/1.2.5",
            "host":"localhost:3000",
            "accept":"*/*"
        }
    },
    "msg":"",
    "time":"2013-10-07T07:53:09.122Z",
    "v":0
}
```

Then it logs the error object, complete with a stack trace (truncated here for sanity):

```
{
    "name":"unnamed app",
    "hostname":"unnamed-host",
    "pid":62136,
    "level":50,
    "err":{
        "message":"Sample error",
        "name":"Error",
        "requestId":"chmhekbuq0001y0ix6k6brxq6",
        "stack":"Error: Sample error
        at createError (/Users/user/Dropbox/dev/
        pja-source/bunyan-request-logger/examples/
        app.js:39:13)
        at ..."
    },
    "msg":"",
    "time":"2013-10-07T07:53:09.124Z",
    "v":0
}
```

Logging the stack trace here could give you a good start on finding the root cause.

Finally, it logs the error response that gets sent to the user:

```
{
    "name":"unnamed app",
    "hostname":"unnamed-host",
    "pid":62136,
    "level":30,
    "res":{
        "statusCode":500,
        "headers":"HTTP/1.1 500 Internal Server
        Error
        X-Powered-By: Express
        Content-Type: text/plain
        Content-Length: 21
        Date: Mon, 07 Oct 2013 07:53:09 GMT
        Connection: keep-alive",
        "requestId":"chmhekbuq0001y0ix6k6brxq6",
        "responseTime":3
    },
    "msg":"",
    "time":"2013-10-07T07:53:09.125Z",
    "v":0
}
```

Logging Service Alerts

All of the services you depend on should be constantly monitored for availability, and
alerts should be configured. When an alert is triggered, the alert should be logged in

addition to having the alert dispatched to the technicians in charge of repairing the service.

Be sure that you're also logging all your service start-ups so that you can also log when the service becomes available again.

Logging Goals

Conversion goals can be measured using tools like Google Analytics without explicitly building the log calls into the source code. You should also log (at a minimum):

- New visitors
- New signups
- Customer transactions
- Application invites

For transactions:

- Timestamp
- User's IP address
- User
- A flag indicating whether the user is a new or repeat customer
- Purchased items
- Total transaction amount
- Entry page
- Keyword used to find the entry page, if any
- Marketing campaign, if known
- Referring user, if known

Most of this data will come from the user session and shopping cart.

Profiling and Instrumentation

It's possible to profile performance and capture errors without explicitly logging all over your codebase. You can instrument code using tools such as New Relic and AppDynamics as a potent supplement to your own log messaging.

Both providers deliver deep insight into the critical performance metrics of your app. New Relic and AppDynamics provide a PaaS service and a freemium model so that you can deploy and evaluate the solution to determine whether or not it will meet your needs before you scale up and pay full price.

New Relic recently developed a Node.js agent, and AppDynamics has acquired Nodetime in order to provide instrumentation for Node.js applications. You should strongly consider instrumentation tools like these before you deploy your production application.

Getting started with New Relic is easy:

```
$ npm install --save newrelic

# assuming ./ is app root
$ cp node_modules/newrelic/newrelic.js ./
```

Edit *newrelic.js* and replace license_key's value with the license key for your account. You might want to replace it with an environment variable so that you can commit the file without committing your key to your application repository.

Add the following as the first line of your app's main module:

```
require('newrelic');
```

The next time you start your app, it will start reporting profiling data.

Similarly, for AppDynamics Nodetime:

```
$ npm install nodetime

require('nodetime').profile({
  accountKey: your_account_key
});
```

Either of these services can show you round-trip times, and Google Analytics can supply timing information as well (under Content → Site Speed).

Logging Client-Side Events

Sometimes actions will occur on the client that you want to keep track of. For those events, it's helpful to establish a log endpoint that simply records all incoming messages. You've already seen how you can do that, simply by logging all incoming requests and then creating a specialized */log.gif* endpoint that doesn't cache and returns a 1 × 1 transparent beacon.

Here's a stripped down implementation, sans error handling:

```
var express = express = require('express'),
  logger = require('../request-logger.js'),
  noCache = require('connect-cache-control'),
  log = logger(),
  app = express(),
  port = 3000;
```

```
app.use( log.requestLogger() );

// Route to handle client-side log messages.
//
// Counter to intuition, client-side logging
// works best with GET requests.
//
// AJAX POST sends headers and body in two steps,
// which slows it down.
//
// This route prepends the cache-control
// middleware so that the browser always logs
// to the server instead of fetching a useless
// No Content message from its cache.
app.get( '/log.gif', noCache, log.route() );

app.listen(port, function () {
  log.info('Listening on port ' + port);
});
```

Deciphering Data

Logs don't do you any good if you have to sift through mountains of data to find the information you're really looking for. It's important to invest in the right tools to help you find the data you need, quickly. Google Analytics provides a lot of data logging, parsing, and visualization out of the box, along with the ability to log custom events, set up custom goals to track, performance profiling, and a lot more. You'll get a lot of actionable data just by adding Google Analytics to your technology mix.

Another great way to gain application insights is to connect your logging mechanisms to data mining tools such as Splunk (*http://www.splunk.com/*), Mixpanel (*https://mixpa nel.com/*), or KISSmetrics (*https://www.kissmetrics.com/*).

Splunk turns mountainous logs into actionable operational intelligence. It can aggregate data from just about any machine-data source, including server logs, network activity, even customer support issues, and phone logs. It has an uncanny ability to make sense of all of it and make it easy to search for data and create detailed reports that allow you to highlight the story that's important to the individual using the data.

For example, the security team can create custom reports that follow an intruder's path spanning multiple systems, while somebody from the marketing is simultaneously looking at a graph of conversion rate changes before and during a promotion.

Mixpanel and KISSmetrics are both focused more specifically on understanding important metrics for web applications. KISSmetrics prides themselves on their ability to give you detailed insights about your customers, while Mixpanel touts the ease of creating and using custom dashboards to track KPIs.

Conclusion

I hope you have a newfound respect for the importance of logging in your application. As you can see, logging can provide a lot of very valuable information.

There is a reason that airplanes have lots of dials on their dashboards. As an ASP, your logging is the nervous system that supplies all of the information for those dials. If you're not delivering actionable data, you're flying blind.

## CHAPTER 8

Building RESTful APIs

What is an API? If you're reading this book, you know that it's an application programming interface, but in the context of a RESTful API, we're specifically talking about an interface that allows users and applications to interact with your application over HTTP using REST architecture (REpresentational State Transfer).

For a very basic overview of REST architecture, see "RESTful JSON Web Services" on page 6. You'll have a chance to explore it in-depth later in this chapter.

Why should you build an API? First of all, you're going to need a way to connect the user interface to your backend resources, like a database, logging services, and maybe some gateways to third-party APIs. But there are good reasons to expose parts of that API to the public as well.

Think carefully about the some of the most successful apps out there: Facebook, Twitter, Google Maps, Amazon (yeah, it's an app—lots of them, actually). I can keep going, but I'd fill the rest of the book with examples. What do all of these have in common?

They all offer public APIs that developers can use to enhance the value of the platform for its users. With a public API, your application is more than an app: it's a platform that other developers will flock to and integrate their apps with. They'll expose your app to new users and make your app more attractive to your existing users, because now it works with other tools that they already use.

But you don't want just any API. You want a beautifully designed API. As Brandon Satrom said at Fluent 2013, "API design is developer UX" (*http://bit.ly/1pFMgaJ*). It's important to be friendly to developers—yourself included.

Your API must be easy to learn, easy to use, easy to explore, and fast.

All of that starts with design. Design should be planned. I don't mean that you should be able to predict the future—only that you should build your API such that it can change over time in ways that are beautiful, not ugly.

So what makes an API beautiful?

Beautiful APIs are:

Usable
> Deliver useful services without confusing users.

Self-describing
> Don't make your API users read the manual; embed the manual in the API.

Efficient
> Bandwidth is expensive. Don't send more data than the user needs.

Responsive
> Make your API respond as quickly as it can.

As you can see, a beautiful API satisfies all of the goals you saw a few paragraphs back:

- Easy to learn: usable, self-describing
- Easy to use: usable, self-describing, efficient
- Easy to explore: self-describing, usable, responsive
- Fast: efficient, responsive

Usable

There are two foundational principles of API design that can help improve the usability of your API and reduce the time it takes for new developers to learn it:

Focus
> The purpose of your API and each API endpoint should be clear, just by interacting with the API.

Consistency
> Each API resource should share the same conventions as the other resources for the same API.

Focus

To focus your API, present only the information your users need and eliminate clutter. If your application is for music lovers, don't provide links to cooking recipes or abstract art.

It sounds easy, but it goes much deeper than that, and a lack of focus plagues many APIs. For example, many endpoints will list nested objects—resources with related data embedded directly in the response. That practice can be convenient, but it can also be confusing. Don't overwhelm API users with gigantic records when they may be looking for a small, specific subset.

For example, consider an API that delivers information about music albums:

```
{
  "id": "chmzq50np0002gfixtr1qp64o",
  "name": "Settle",
  "artist": {
    "id": "chmzq4l480001gfixe8a3nzhm",
    "name": "Disclosure",
    "tourDates": [
      {
        "id": "chmzq45yn0000gfixa0wj6z9j",
        "date": "Sat Oct 19 2013",
        "name": "Treasure Island Music Festival",
        "location": "San Francisco, CA, US",
        "attending": [
          {
            "id": "chmzq7tyj0003gfix0rcylkls",
            "name": "Guy Lawrence"
          },
          {
            "id": "chmzqougy0004gfixuk66lhv4",
            "name": "Howard Lawrence"
          }
        ]
      }
    ]
  },
  "...": "..."
}
```

If all the user is looking for is a list of album titles and artist names, this is going to be overload. Instead of this, you can *focus* on the particular information that your users are most likely to need. Of course you should make it easy for them to get more if they want it, too. Just make the default sensible.

Take a look at this version and see if it makes more sense:

```
{
  "id": "chmzq50np0002gfixtr1qp64o",
  "name": "Settle",
  "artist": "Disclosure",
  "artistId": "chmzq4l480001gfixe8a3nzhm",
  "coverImage": "/covers/medium/zrms5gxr.jpg",
  "year": "2013",
  "genres": [
    "electronic", "house", "garage", "UK garage",
    "future garage"
  ]
}
```

Instead of inlining a bunch of completely unrelated data about the artist, you get the artist name (which you'll likely need to display in any album listing) and an ID you can use to query more information about the artist if it's needed.

The listing now is focused on the particular resource that's being queried right now: the *album*. Focus may be the most important principle of good UX, whether you're designing the UI for a shopping cart or the shopping cart's API.

Consistency

Consistency is all about letting users build on prior knowledge while they learn how to use your service. Once they learn how to complete one task, they should be able to apply that learning to the next task. You can make your learning curve a lot easier to climb by making your API as consistent as possible.

There are a couple of great ways to do that with a RESTful API:

- Use standard REST conventions.
- Adopt a style for your API endpoints, and stick to that same style for every endpoint (including errors).

Use common conventions

A lot of consistency is built into the REST architecture. Sticking to the conventions of REST can go a long way toward making your API more consistent, both internally and with other APIs that the users might be familiar with.

A defining characteristic is that REST does not deal with remote procedure calls (RPC). Instead, it is only concerned with the transfer of state. The difference is verbs versus nouns. When you call a procedure, you're asking the API to *do* something. When you transfer state, you're sharing data *about* something. RPC is *control oriented*, while REST is *data oriented*.

The advantage of a data-oriented architecture style is that it can map to any domain without embedding knowledge of the particular domain in the client. In other words, everything you need to know to interact successfully with a RESTful API should be contained in:

1. The protocol(s) (HTTP URIs, GET, POST, etc.)
2. The media type (rules for interpreting messages)
3. The messages from the server (hyperlinks, templates, etc.)

The goal of REST is to avoid coupling the client application and the server application. In fact, successful REST clients should be able to browse completely unrelated RESTful

APIs. The most obvious example is the web browser. It doesn't know anything about a website until you browse to it and start to explore the hyperlinks contained in the requested document. An example of a generic JSON hypermedia browsing client is Jsonary (*http://jsonary.com/*).

That consistency is useful for more than usability. It's also great for application maintainability, because it decouples your client application from your server application such that changes to your API can be published without breaking existing clients.

One requirement of REST is that you respect the methods defined by the protocol. With few exceptions (such as the /log.gif tracking pixel hack covered in "Logging Requests" on page 156), the HTTP methods should be respected by your API. Don't use GET when you really mean POST or PUT. Exceptions should be practical workarounds for problems such as holes in specifications or implementations, and those workarounds should be made with the expectation that they will eventually be obsolete.

For example, HTML forms only support GET and POST methods, so if you want to allow users to access other features of your API without using JavaScript, you'll need to make some practical concessions.

Here's another example: many users are still using IE 8, and most of us still need to support it. IE 8 supports PATCH, but only via the proprietary ActiveXObject for XMLHTTP.

One popular workaround that can solve both the HTML form and IE 8 PATCH problem is to implement method override.

Method override works by passing an X-HTTP-Method-Override header (a common convention), or an optional _method key set to the method you wish to emulate in your request. So, if you want to PUT a record using an HTML form, simply POST the form with _methdod parameter set to PUT. If you want to use PATCH, you can set the X-HTTP-Method-Override and POST the contents.

Express can automatically check for a method override setting and route the request to the appropriate method handler. To make that happen, use the connect methodOverr ide middleware:

```
// You need to parse the body to get the method param:
app.use( express.json() );
app.use( express.urlencoded() );

// Now methodOverride() will work:
app.use( express.methodOverride() );
```

The really important thing to get right is that you honor the correct methods for clients that support them. That way, modern clients can consistently do things the right way, while methodOverride() provides a fallback for legacy clients.

Another comment about methods: If your server supports any methods for a given resource, it should deliver a 405 Method Not Allowed error as opposed to a 404 Not Found error for all the other methods. If your API and your documentation says that an endpoint is there, but the user gets a 404 Not Found error, that's confusing. Luckily, Express makes this easy:

```
app.get( '/albums', albumHandler() );
app.all('/albums', function (req, res, next) {
  var err = new Error();
  err.route = '/albums';
  err.status = 405;
  next(err);
});
```

If you're using an error-handler middleware that will catch all your routing errors and deliver appropriate error messages (see "Logging Errors" on page 160), you're in business. Otherwise, you could do this instead (not recommended):

```
app.get( '/albums', albumHandler() );
app.all('/albums', function (req, res, next) {
  res.send(405);
});
```

The disadvantage of the latter approach is that if you later want to add support for custom JSON responses for errors to add helpful links to working methods, you'll have to find every route endpoint that did its own error handling and update them one at a time.

Another serious problem with both of the previous examples is that they return a Content-Type: text/plain header. Since you're building an API that works on the *application/json* media type, that inconsistency will be confusing to your users.

If you use the express-error-handler module in discussed the section on error handling, there's a lot less to remember:

```
app.get( '/albums', albumHandler() );
app.all( '/albums', errorHandler.httpError(405) );
```

This will deliver the 405 message in *application/json*.

In the context of a simple albums service, complete with proper error handling and logging, it might look something like this:

```
'use strict';

var express = require('express'),
  http = require('http'),
  logger = require('bunyan-request-logger'),
  errorHandler = require('express-error-handler'),
  app = express(),
  log = logger(),
  server,
  port = 3000;
```

```
app.use( express.json() );
app.use( express.urlencoded() );
app.use( express.methodOverride() );
app.use( log.requestLogger() );

// Respond to get requests on /albums
app.get('/albums', function (req, res) {
  res.send({
    chmzq50np0002gfixtr1qp64o: {
      "id": "chmzq50np0002gfixtr1qp64o",
      "name": "Settle",
      "artist": "Disclosure",
      "artistId": "chmzq4l480001gfixe8a3nzhm",
      "coverImage": "/covers/medium/zrms5gxr.jpg",
      "year": "2013",
      "genres": [
        "electronic", "house", "garage", "UK garage",
        "future garage"
      ]
    }
  });
});

// Deliver 405 errors if the request method isn't
// defined.
app.all( '/albums', errorHandler.httpError(405) );


// Deliver 404 errors for any unhandled routes.
// Express has a 404 handler built-in, but it
// won't deliver errors consistent with your API.
app.all( '*', errorHandler.httpError(404) );

// Log errors.
app.use( log.errorLogger() );

// Create the server
server = http.createServer(app);

// Handle errors. Remember to pass the server
// object into the error handler, so it can be
// shut down gracefully in the event of an
// unhandled error.
app.use( errorHandler({
  server: server
}) );

server.listen(port, function () {
  console.log('Listening on port ' + port);
});
```

Resourceful routing

Imagine we're talking about the process of adding new album cover art to an albums collection, and the UI exposes a way for you to select an album cover via HTTP. The server goes and fetches the image from the URL, encodes it, and adds the resized/encoded image to the album record. Instead of exposing an /encode-image endpoint, you could PUT to the /albums endpoint:

PUT /albums/123:

```
{
  "coverSourceURL":
    "http://cdn2.pitchfork.com/news/50535/f40d167d.jpg",
  "id": "chmzq50np0002gfixtr1qp64o",
  "name": "Settle",
  "artist": "Disclosure",
  "artistId": "chmzq4l480001gfixe8a3nzhm",
  "year": "2013",
  "genres": [
    "electronic", "house", "garage", "UK garage",
    "future garage"
  ]
}
```

The route can check for the existence of the coverSourceURL, fetch it, process the image, and replace the key with:

```
"coverImage": "/covers/medium/zrms5gxr.jpg"
```

Resources describe your data, represented by nouns, and HTTP provides the verbs to manipulate the nouns. You might remember the basic set of manipulations from Chapter 1:

- Create a new entry in the resource collection: HTTP POST.
- Retrieve a resource representation: HTTP GET verb.
- Update (replace) the resource: HTTP PUT.
- Delete a resource: HTTP DELETE.

That leaves out PATCH, which has been supported in most major browsers since IE 7, though you'll need the methodOverride() hack mentioned before.

CRUD has long been a convenient way to deal with records, but maybe it has outlived its usefulness as the default way to manipulate state.

It's a really simplistic way of viewing the REST architecture, and perhaps not the best way. For instance, PUT is often used for resource creation.

The major advantage of PUT is that it's idempotent. If you PUT the same resource twice, it doesn't change anything. The classic example is a shopping cart order. If you POST a shopping cart order, and POST again, it will trigger two different checkouts. That's probably not what the user wants. That's why you'll see warning messages if you POST something and then hit the back button. Browsers will warn that the data will be posted again. If you're building the server implementation, it's your job to enforce idempotency for PUT operations.

PUT can also help you build applications that are capable of functioning offline. To do that, you need to be able to create a complete record on the client side, without the need to connect to the server first to retrieve the ID for a newly created record. Using PUT for resource creation can also impact the perceived performance of the app. If users don't have to wait for a spinner every time they create something, they're going to have a much smoother experience.

Of course, you'll still want to validate all the data that the client eventually sends. Just do it as soon as you can, and deal with the errors as the app becomes aware of them. Being able to gracefully resolve data conflicts is becoming a necessary part of application design as realtime collaboration features find their way into a growing number of apps.

A resource is just a collection of related data, such as the /albums endpoint mentioned before. Routing for the resource could be mapped as follows (opinions differ on the correct mapping):

```
GET     /albums             -> index
POST    /albums             -> create, return URI
GET     /albums/:id         -> show
PUT     /albums/:id         -> create or update
DELETE  /albums/:id         -> destroy
```

Start by making the index route behave more like an index:

```
// GET     /albums     -> index
app.get('/albums', function (req, res) {
  var index = map(albums, function (album) {
    return {
      href: '/albums/' + album.id,
      properties: {
        name: album.name,
        artist: album.artist
      }
    };
  });
  res.send(index);
});
```

That slims it down a little:

```
{
  "chmzq50np0002gfixtr1qp64o": {
    "href": "/albums/chmzq50np0002gfixtr1qp64o",
    "properties": {
      "name": "Settle",
```

```
      "artist": "Disclosure"
    }
  }
}
```

Support POST:

```
// POST    /albums    -> create, return URI
app.post('/albums', function (req, res) {
  var id = cuid(),
    album = mixIn({}, req.body, {
      id: id
    });

  albums[id] = album;
  res.send(201, {
    href: '/albums/' + id
  });
});
```

Deliver helpful messages for the /albums index:

```
// Send available options on OPTIONS requests
app.options( '/albums', function (req, res) {
  res.send(['GET', 'POST', 'OPTIONS']);
});

// Deliver 405 errors if the request method isn't
// defined.
app.all( '/albums', errorHandler.httpError(405) );
```

Allow users to get more detail for a particular album:

```
// GET    /albums/:id    ->    show
app.get('/albums/:id', function (req, res, next) {
  var id = req.params.id,
    body = albums[id],
    err;

  if (!body) {
    err = new Error('Album not found');
    err.status = 404;
    return next(err);
  }

  res.send(200, body);
});
```

Allow users to PUT complete albums with a client-generated ID:

```
// PUT    /albums/:id    -> create or update
app.put('/albums/:id', function (req, res) {
  var album = mixIn({}, req.body),
    id = req.params.id,
    exists = albums[id];
```

```
    album.id = id;
    albums[id] = album;

    if (exists) {
      return res.send(204);
    }

    res.send(201, {
      href: '/albums/' + album.id
    });
  });
```

Your users need a way to delete albums:

```
// DELETE   /albums/:id    -> destroy
app.delete('/albums/:id',
    function (req, res, next) {
  var id = req.params.id,
    body = albums[id],
    err;

  if (!body) {
    err = new Error('Album not found');
    err.status = 404;
    return next(err);
  }

  delete albums[id];

  res.send(204);
});
```

The *albums/:id* endpoint needs its own helpful errors:

```
// Send available options on OPTIONS requests
app.options( '/albums', function (req, res) {
  res.send(['GET', 'PUT', 'DELETE', 'OPTIONS']);
});

// 405 Method Not Allowed
app.all( '/albums/:id', errorHandler.httpError(405) );
```

That should get you started. A lot of people think that if they've got this far, they've created a RESTful API. It's RESTish, but remember that list of goals from before:

- Easy to learn: usable, self-describing
- Easy to use: usable, self-describing, efficient
- Easy to explore: self-describing, usable, responsive
- Fast: efficient, responsive

It's RESTish and resourceful, but there's one more important step you need to take to satisfy those goals: it needs to be self-describing.

Self-Describing: Hypermedia

Hypertext is a text-based resource with embedded references to other text resources. Hypermedia applies the concept to rich media resources, such as images, video, and audio. The Web started out as a system built on hypertext resources, and has since evolved into a system built on hypermedia resources.

Affordances

> When I say Hypertext, I mean the simultaneous presentation of information and controls such that the information becomes the affordance through which the user obtains choices and selects actions.
>
> —Roy T. Fielding

Affordances are all of the possible actions you can perform on a resource. In the context of hypermedia, an affordance might be a link for clicking or a form to manipulate the resource. The buttons on your keyboard afford pressing. The mouse affords cursor movement, and so on.

Roy Fielding envisioned an architectural style whereby all affordances for an API are delivered by means of hypermedia.

Mike Amundsen took that a step further and specified nine different affordances that document aspects of state transitions over the network (described in much more detail in his book, *Building Hypermedia APIs with HTML5 and Node* [O'Reilly, 2011]). He calls them H-Factors and breaks them down into two categories:

1. Link support:

   [LE] *Embedding links*
   Fetch a linked resource and embed it into the current resource

   [LO] *Outbound links*
   Create links that causes navigation to another resource

   [LT] *Templated queries*
   Communicate to the client how to query a resource

   [LN] *Non-idempotent updates*
   Update that will cause state changes if repeated (aka, unsafe updates; for example, POST)

[LI] *Idempotent updates*
Update that will not cause state changes if repeated (aka, safe updates; for example, PUT)

2. Control data support:

[CR] *Modify control data for read requests*
For example, HTTP Accept-* headers

[CU] *Modify control data for update requests*
For example, HTTP Content-* headers

[CM] *Modify control data for interface methods*
For example, select between POST and PUT

[CL] *Modify control data for links*
Add semantic meaning to links (relations); for example, rel attribute

HTML actually has a couple other important affordances worth mentioning that are not members of the aforementioned transition-focused H-Factors:

Specify presentation rules
For example, CSS

Specify behavior
Code on demand (see Roy Fielding's famous REST Dissertation (*http://www.ics.uci.edu/~fielding/pubs/dissertation/top.htm*), "Architectural Styles and the Design of Network-based Software Architectures"); for example, JavaScript

The more affordances a media type provides, the closer you can get to HATEOAS.

HATEOAS

HATEOAS (Hypermedia As The Engine Of Application State) is an important but often overlooked method of improving an API. Essentially, it means that your server gives the client the information it needs to interact with your API so that the client doesn't have to remember out-of-band information, like endpoint URLs, data formats, available features, etc.:

> All application state transitions must be driven by client selection of server-provided choices that are present in the received representations or implied by the user's manipulation of those representations [...] Failure here implies that out-of-band information is driving interaction instead of hypertext.
>
> —From the blog post "REST APIs must be Hypertext Driven" by Roy T. Fielding (*http://bit.ly/roy-gbiv-restAPIs*)

The idea is to decouple the client from the server so that they are literally two completely independent applications. There are several advantages:

- Your API is more browsable and self-documenting.
- You can upgrade or make changes to your API at any time without breaking clients, and all clients will receive the changes automatically.
- Reduce long-term maintenance costs. The more clients assume about your API, the more logic you'll need to support changes you make to the API.
- Clients are more adaptable to temporary changes; for example, if a host becomes unreachable, you can update the URI in your hyperlinks.
- You can use the presence or lack of links in place of a traditional feature toggle system. In other words, all client features exist because the RESTful service informs the client that the features exist.

A good rule of thumb to achieve this level of affordance in your API is to write a client test implementation in parallel with your API design, and see if your client can do everything it needs to do following one simple rule:

Code to the media type, not to the message.

What does that mean? It means that your client should be aware of the rules for interpreting the messages, but not aware of the contents of the messages themselves. If you can successfully build your app with that restriction, you can achieve a high degree of loose coupling, which will make your client very responsive to API changes.

The primary disadvantages are:

- Developer education and compliance. Once you deliver a link to clients, it's hard to prevent them from embedding that link in their applications.
- Efficiency. If you have to make a call to get a link to make another call, you pay for two server round trips instead of one.

The first issue can be managed by writing good SDKs for resource consumers. If the SDKs wrap your API and comply with the best practices of the API, and consumers have incentive to use the SDK (because presumably, it makes working with your API easier), that can go a long way.

The second can be managed by making affordances in your API that allow clients to discover resources efficiently and cache URLs on the client side so that they don't have to look them up every time they need access to a particular resource. That process can also be aided with a good SDK.

One of the great advantages of a truly HATEOAS API is that a single SDK could be used to power any number of different API services across an organization. It should even be possible to create a client SDK that works for any system that happens to rely on the same hypermedia type, provided that the target APIs make enough affordances.

HTML as an API Media Type

Recently, more adventurous API designers have been experimenting with using HTML instead of JSON-based media types to communicate with their APIs. The thinking is that HTML powers the biggest success case of the REST architectural style and already supports many features that are missing from many other hypermedia types, including the ability to include JavaScript and style the output so that it's easier for humans to view.

An interesting perspective on this topic is that the website and the API could literally be the same thing, as long as you're careful to embed enough affordances in the HTML to serve the needs of your developers.

This isn't a terrible idea, but I think that HTML is a little too verbose for this purpose. HTML also lacks a couple of key affordances, as you'll see in a minute. There is a possible alternative.

Jade

Jade was designed as a minimal template markup that you can use to generate HTML. It offers a lighter weight, more convenient syntax, while retaining the expressive power of HTML.

Here's how you might represent the */albums* collection (minus some navigation links, for brevity):

```
head
  title Order
body.order
  h1 Order
  ul.properties
    li.property
      label Order Number
        span.orderNumber 42
    li.property
      label Item Count
        span.itemCount 3
    li.property
      label Status
        span.status pending

  ul.entities
    li.entity.items.collection
      a(rel='http://x.io/rels/order-items',
        href='http://api.x.io/orders/42/items')
        | Items

    li.entity.info.customer
      a(rel='http://x.io/rels/customer'
        href='http://api.x.io/customers/pj123'),
```

```
          ul.properties
            li.property
              label Customer ID
                span.customerId pj123
            li.property
              label Name
                span.name Peter Joseph

      ul.actions
        li.action
          // Action is one of:
          // index, create, show, put, delete, patch
          // The method in html is determined by the
          // mapping between actions and HTML methods.
          form(action='create',
            href='http://api.x.io/orders/42/items',
            type='application/x-www-form-urlencoded')
            fieldset
              legend Add Item
              label Order Number
                input(name='orderNumber', hidden='hidden', value='42')
              label Product Code
                input(name='productCode', type='text')
              label Quantity
                input(name='quantity', type='number')

    ul.links
      a(rel='self', href='http://api.x.io/orders/42',
        style='display: none;')
      a(rel='previous', href='http://api.x.io/orders/41') Previous
      a(rel='next', href='http://api.x.io/orders/43') Next
```

Here's the equivalent HTML:

```
<head profile="http://ericelliott.me/profiles/resource">
    <title>Albums</title>
</head>

<body class="albums">
    <h1 class="title">Albums</h1>

    <ul class="properties">
        <li class="property">
            <p class="description">A list of albums you should listen to.</p>
        </li>

        <li class="property"><!-- A count of the total number of entities-->
        <!-- available. Useful for paging info.-->
        <label for="entityCount">Total count:</label> <span class="entityCount"
        id="entityCount">3</span></li>
    </ul>

    <ul class="entities">
```

```
        <li class="entity album">
            <a href="/albums/a65x0qxr" rel="item">
            <ul class="properties">
                <li class="property name">Dark Side of the Moon</li>

                <li class="property artist">Pink Floyd</li>
            </ul></a>
        </li>

        <li class="entity album">
            <a href="/albums/a7ff1qxw" rel="item">
            <ul class="properties">
                <li class="property name">Random Access Memories</li>

                <li class="property artist">Daft Punk</li>
            </ul></a>
        </li>
    </ul>

    <ul class="links">
        <li class="link">
            <a href="/albums?offset=2&amp;limit=1" rel="next">Next</a>
        </li>

        <li class="link">
            <link href="http://albums.com/albums" rel="self, canonical">
        </li>
    </ul>
</body>
```

Jiron

Jiron is a hypermedia type inspired by Siren that extends it with the semantics of HTML. The Jade-only version is missing a couple of important affordances:

- Idempotent updates [LI], and
- Control data for reads [CR]

However, Jiron can fix both issues:

Starting with the idempotent updates, imagine the following syntax:

```
form(method='put', href="/names/123")
    label(for='name')
    input#name
```

which maps to the broken HTML:

```
<form method="PUT" href="/names/123">
    <label for="name"></label>
    <input id="name"/>
</form>
```

You'll need a media type that includes information that allows your client to handle such requests. Imagine that your client is built to handle all requests via Ajax. It intercepts them all, grabs the method parameter, and passes it through to the server without examining it (trusting the server to validate it).

Now, any method supported by the server will be supported by both the media type and the client, automatically.

Great! Now you need a way to ask the server for this new media type in your links. No problem:

```
a(headers='Accept:application/vnd.jiron+jade') Some Jiron resource
```

And the HTML (again, this won't work with vanilla HTML):

```
<a headers="Accept:application/vnd.jiron+jade">Some Jiron resource</a>
```

This allows you to pass arbitrary headers when you click on links. The client will intercept all link activations and serve the links via Ajax.

Take another look at that earlier /albums example. That isn't any ordinary HTML. It contains class and rel attributes that obviously have some semantic meaning. That's because it's actually based on Siren+JSON. It's a mapping of Siren entity semantics on to HTML documents and ul elements.

Here are some things you can do with Jiron that you can't do with JSON:

- Deliver code on demand with JavaScript links (including any client SDK you need to customize any Jiron browser for your particular API)
- Deliver default templates that make browsing your API directly in a browser pleasant
- Deliver clickable links and usable forms while your users are browsing the API directly
- Use CSS for styling default views
- Intersperse human-readable text and media with hypertext controls and affordances—like HTML, only structured specifically for APIs

And stuff you can't do with HTML:

- Support any method type. PUT, PATCH, DELETE? No problem.
- Support header changes in links.

Since Jiron is based on the existing Jade HTML template syntax, the documents are easy to interpret with existing Jade tools and browser tools. Browserify users can use *https:// github.com/substack/node-jadeify*. You can also use Browserify to export an AMD module or standalone module for the browser if you don't want to use Browserify for module management in the client.

Using it in the browser is simple:

```
jade.render('a.album(href="/albums/123") Pretty Hate Machine');
```

which creates the string:

```
<a href="/albums/123" class="album">Pretty Hate Machine</a>
```

Now you can add that to a documentFragment and use CSS selectors to query it. Better yet, just slap some CSS on it and render it as-is. Try that with JSON.

Even if you use Jiron, you'll still be sending data to the server using URL parameters and JSON bodies. Those formats are universally understood by web servers, and that will save you the trouble of parsing Jiron documents on the server side.

If you want to support the application/vnd.jiron+html type, or Jiron over *text/html*, just process the Jade template on the server before you send it to the client.

Responsive APIs

Different API consumers have different needs. One way to make your API more valuable is to make it responsive to those different, often conflicting needs. You can enable a more responsive API by looking at request parameters and changing the output based on the user's requests. Here is a list of commonly supported request options:

Accept
    Allow users to request alternative content types. At a minimum, make it possible to add them later.

Embed
    Retrieve and embed related entities in place:

```
# Get all albums, embed artist representations
# in the response.
GET /albums?embed=artist
```

Sideline
    Another way to include related entities. Like embedding, only the resource link is left in the original resource. For sidelining, the linked resource is included in the returned collection as a top-level element that can be retrieved by keyed lookup:

```
# Fetch the artist represented by the
# `artist` rel in the album `links`
# collection.
GET /albums?sideline=artist
```

Sort

Different applications will have different requirements for sorting complexity, but most should support basic sorting:

```
# Sort albums by year, oldest to newest
GET /albums?sort=year+asc

# Sort albums by artist, alphabetical
GET /albums?sort=artist+asc

# Sort albums by year, newest to oldest, then album name, alphabetical
GET /albums?sort=year+desc,name+asc
```

Paging

Remember to return relevant links, such as previous/next/first/last:

```
GET /albums?offset=10&limit=10
# Or...
GET /albums?page=2&limit=10
```

Fields

Send only the fields specified. The default response should just set defaults for the fields param:

```
GET /albums?fields=name,year,artist
```

Filter

Show only the results matching the given filter criteria:

```
GET /albums?artist="Disclosure"

# Get albums from all these years:
GET /albums?year=1969,1977,1983,1994,1998,2013

# Get albums from any of these years with the keyword "EP":
GET /albums?year=1969,1977,1983,1994,1998,2013;keyword=EP

# Get all albums except those with genre=country:
GET /albums?genre=!country
```

This is an area where the tooling for Node could use a lot of improvement. Some early-stage projects worth following include:

- Fortune (*http://fortunejs.com/*)
- Percolator (*http://percolatorjs.com/*)
- siren-resource (*https://github.com/dilvie/siren-resource*)

Most of the examples in this chapter were generated using siren-resource. It was written for that purpose, but it supports some interesting features that the others lack, and I literally took the bullet points right off the siren-resource roadmap (*https://github.com/dilvie/siren-resource/issues?milestone=1&state=open*).

Optimizing for Speed

You can have the best API design in the world, but if it's too slow, nobody will want to use it. Here are some quick tips to keep things moving quickly:

- Store all commonly viewed resources and queries in an in-memory cache. Consider Redis (*http://redis.io/*) or Memcached (*http://memcached.org/*)

- Make sure your cache headers and ETags are set properly for all cacheable resources.

- Make sure you're compressing your resource endpoints. See the `express.com press()` or equivalent middleware.

- Use paging. Make it automatic on every resource, and make sure there is a maximum page size enforced.

- Stream large responses so that user agents can start processing it as soon as possible.

- Index any keys that are commonly used for filtering and searching.

- Limit access to queries that require processing time.

- Avoid making unnecessary network calls. If you can colocate backend services and side-band resources on the same server, you'll trim a lot of latency.

- Avoid making unnecessary IPC calls. If you can accomplish in a library what you have been doing in a separate process, do it, unless doing so could slow down the event loop.

- Avoid blocking. Always use the asynchronous versions of Node function calls during request and response cycles. The only times you should consider synchronous versions are for application startup and command-line utilities.

- Always use nonblocking algorithms for query processing. Don't process large collections with synchronous iterator functions. Consider time slicing or workers instead.

- Take advantage of load balancing to spread the load across multiple CPU cores. The cluster module or HAProxy (*http://haproxy.1wt.eu/*) should do the trick. As of this writing, HAProxy handles it better, but the cluster module is undergoing a rewrite to improve its performance.

- Offload all static assets to CDNs.

- Profile your app performance. Use an app monitoring tool like New Relic (*http://newrelic.com/*) to detect potential issues.

- Load test your application. Carefully monitor latency and memory use characteristics under strain.

Conclusion

This chapter could have been a whole book on its own. I could not possibly tell you everything you need to know about building an API to prepare you for large-scale production within the scope of this book, but hopefully you have been introduced to most of the key concepts, and you at least know which keywords to Google for if you want to learn more.

Here is a list of best practices you may want to refer back to:

- Use consistent routing.
- Use hypermedia as the engine of application state.
- Program to the media type, not to the API data.
- Use a media type that supports the right number and right type of affordances (H-Factors) for your application.
- Consider the benefits of using an HTML-based media type.

The UX is the soul of an application; the API is the heart. Take the time to make sure your application has a good one. Your users will love you for it.

## CHAPTER 9

Feature Toggle

Continuous deployment is the process of testing, integrating, and deploying software in rapid cycles in order to deliver bug fixes and new features to customers as quickly as possible. It gained popular acceptance as a cornerstone of extreme programming and agile development and is very popular among Software as a Service providers.

A *feature toggle* system allows you to integrate features into your codebase even before they're finished and ready to release. During development, the features are toggled off by default. In order to turn them on, you must enable them manually. Using this method, you can deploy unfinished or untested changes into your production system without interfering with the user experience.

Feature toggles can allow software integration cycles that run in weeks, days, or even hours, as opposed to months or years. They are an essential component in a broader continuous integration system.

Feature toggles are popular in the startup community but have gained widespread acceptance in the enterprise, including larger companies such as Facebook, Google, Yahoo, and Adobe.

Organizing Features

Deciding how to organize features begins with deciding what exactly constitutes a feature. Once you figure that out, you should also decide how you're going to classify or group features together.

Scale of a Feature

"Feature" can mean almost anything, ranging from a new page or route to an additional option on a `select` element. Deciding how to classify the scope of the feature is up to the project manager, but it's easy to go overboard with features. My recommendation is to toggle at the page/route level whenever possible.

Features should be toggled on and off at the largest scale possible. For example, if you're building a new page, you shouldn't check whether the feature is on for every operation used to build up the page. Instead, toggle the feature at the route level. If the feature is a new element on the page, create a new view for that element, and only render that view if the feature is toggled on.

APIs should also use a feature toggle system, and the API should be capable of toggling at the route level, as well.

If you happen to use a hypermedia API and hypermedia-aware client, you can turn features on and off in the client simply by adding or removing resources from the API. For example, if you want to disable a route, just remove it from your hypermedia links, and the client won't be able to discover and use the route.

Feature Groups

Sometimes it's handy to group features together. You should definitely do so for features that are designed to interact with each other. For instance, you might have a user ratings feature that allows users to add stars and comments to items in a list. The stars and comments are both subfeatures of the user-ratings parent feature. If ratings are turned off, users can no longer comment or add stars to an item. It's possible to build a feature-dependency graph to keep track of which features rely on each other to operate correctly, and then toggle them on and off simultaneously.

Groups can also be handy for marketing purposes. Sometimes it's useful to group several exciting new features together into a newsworthy release. For products that rely on publicity cycles to spur growth, engineering must provide the technical capabilities to generate worthy news events.

It's essential for the product team to engage the marketing team in a realistic way. The executives and marketing department should not start touting a release date until the features are in the testing stage and nearing completion. Features don't need to be released the moment they're complete. You can hold completed features for a scheduled marketing event and flip the toggle switch at the precise moment that marketing has promised delivery. Since the features are already deployed into production, they'll be live and ready to use immediately.

Features are often grouped in default sets for each environment, as well. A default set commonly includes all of the features that will be toggled on in the next deploy cycle.

Lifespan of a Feature

The creation of a feature begins with naming and documentation. Before you write a line of code, name and describe the feature, along with any required criteria to qualify it for production activation. "User ratings" might be a good feature name.

Development

Start with a few unit tests. What does the feature do? How can you verify that behavior with code? For example, "A user should be able to give an item a star rating," and, "A user should be able to comment on an item." Once that's done, begin the implementation. You can hide features with CSS or by wrapping the lines of code that trigger the feature in a conditional block that only executes if the feature is enabled.

Staging

At the staging phase, features can be toggled on or off. Generally, the next set of production deploy defaults will be toggled on by default in staging. Developers and QA teams can toggle on individual features to verify that they work correctly and interact well with other features.

With the user-ratings feature, testers can toggle on just the comments, just the star ratings, or both, and make sure that everything works as expected regardless of the feature configuration. One reason it's important to lifespan feature toggles is that the various combinations of feature sets can quickly proliferate, and testing the various combinations can become unmanageable.

Some apps have feature toggle consoles that can be accessed by authorized users in staging and production. This can be a good strategy to enable manual testing. It's also common to enable clients to toggle features on and off using query parameters in order to facilitate automated testing.

Production Testing

Using feature toggles, it's possible to test new features in production without affecting the experience of regular users. It's important to run another battery of tests after you have deployed features to production, and if a feature remains toggled off for very long before rollout, the smoke screen tests should be repeated again just prior to rollout.

Feature Rollout

Once features have been thoroughly tested in staging and production environments, they can be gradually rolled out to a percent of the general user population. You can start with 10% and gradually increase it. Be sure to track critical metrics during the rollout, and be prepared to roll back feature toggles that have an adverse effect on critical metrics.

It's possible that simple star ratings could improve metrics, but comments could add clutter and distraction. Rolling features out gradually allows you to assess the impact on the overall user experience without taking a big loss if something doesn't work out as expected.

Default Activation

Default activation means that the feature is active by default across the whole system, and not on a user-by-user basis. A feature can stay in this state until it is no longer needed or until it is phased out, or it can progress to full integration status.

After seeing the results from the percentage rollout, you might want to make star ratings default while you try to refine the user experience for comments.

Full Integration

Once a feature has made it this far, it's time to remove the feature toggle from the source code and the feature name from the features database. Cleaning up feature branching will reduce code complexity and make it easier to maintain the code going forward.

At this point, you would remove the conditional code around both the user ratings top-level feature and the star ratings. You'll still have feature toggle code for comments until you find a way to integrate them without hurting the user experience.

Implementation

On the client side, you can show and hide features based on the presence of CSS classes. Take the following HTML:

```
<!DOCTYPE html>
<html>
  <head>
    <title>Feature Toggle Demo</title>
    <style>
      li {
        display: inline-block;
        margin-left: 1em;
      }

      .new-feature {
        display: none;
      }

      .ft-new-feature .new-feature {
        display: inline-block;
```

```
        }
      </style>
    </head>
    <body>
      <p>Add <code>?ft=new-feature</code> to the end
        of the url to see the new feature.</p>
      <div class="menu">
        <ul>
          <li class="old-feature">Boring old feature</li>
          <li class="new-feature">New feature!</li>
        </ul>
      </div>
      <script src="../dist/feature-toggle-client.js">
      </script>
      <script>
        // Activate the feature toggle system.
        var ft = featureToggle();
      </script>
    </body>
  </html>
```

By setting the `.ft-new-feature` class on the body tag, you can make the feature show up in the menu. Here's a client-side script that can manage feature toggles in the browser:

```
'use strict';

var union = require('mout/array/union'),
  contains = require('mout/array/contains'),
  EventEmitter = require('events').EventEmitter,
  stampit = require('stampit'),

  /**
   * Grab the url parameters and build a map of
   * parameter names and values.
   * @return {Object} params object
   */
  getParams = function getParams() {
    var params = {};
    if (location.search) {
      var parts = location.search.slice(1).split('&');

      parts.forEach(function (part) {
        var pair = part.split('=');
        pair[0] = decodeURIComponent(pair[0]);
        pair[1] = decodeURIComponent(pair[1]);
        params[pair[0]] = (pair[1] !== 'undefined') ?
          pair[1] : true;
      });
    }
    return params;
  },

  /**
```

```
 * Get a list of feature names from the url
 * parameters.
 * @return {Array} Features list
 */
getParamFeatures = function getParamFeatures() {
  var features = getParams().ft;
  return features ? features.split(',') : undefined;
},

/**
 * Combine the list of base features with
 * the features passed in via URL parameters.
 * @type {Array} active features
 */
getActiveFeatures =
    function getActiveFeatures(baseFeatures,
      paramFeatures) {
  return union(baseFeatures, paramFeatures);
},

/**
 * Takes an array of features and creates a class for
 * each of them on the body tag.
 * New features should be hidden in CSS by default
 * and revealed only when the feature toggle is set:
 *
 * .new-feature { display: none; }
 * .ft-new-feature .new-feature { display: block; }
 *
 * @param {Array} features An array of active features.
 */
setFlags = function setFlags(features) {
  var featureClasses = features.map(function (feature) {
      return 'ft-' + feature;
    }).join(' '),
    classNames = document.getElementsByTagName('body')[0]
      .className.split(' ').filter(function (className) {
        return !className.match(/^ft/);
      });
  document.getElementsByTagName('body')[0].className =
    classNames.join(' ') + ' ' + featureClasses;
},

/**
 * Take an optional list of features, set the feature
 * classes on the body tag, and return the feature
 * toggle object.
 * @param {Array} baseFeatures List of base features.
 * @return {Object} feature object
 */
setFeatures = function setFeatures(baseFeatures) {
  var paramFeatures = getParamFeatures(),
```

```
activeFeatures = getActiveFeatures(baseFeatures,
  paramFeatures),

methods = {
  /**
   * Check to see if a feature is active.
   * @param  {String} feature
   * @return {Boolean}
   */
  active: function active(feature) {
    var testFeature = feature && feature.trim &&
      feature.trim();
    return contains(activeFeatures, testFeature);
  },

  /**
   * Activate a list of features.
   * @emits activated
   * @param  {Array} features
   * @return {Object} this (for chaining)
   */
  /**
   * activated event.
   *
   * @event activated
   * @type {Array} activated features
   */
  activate: function activate(features) {
    activeFeatures = union(activeFeatures, features);
    setFlags(activeFeatures);
    this.emit('activated', features);
    return this;
  },

  /**
   * Deactivate a list of features.
   * @emits deactivated
   * @param  {Array} features
   * @return {Object} this (for chaining)
   */
  /**
   * deactivated event.
   *
   * @event deactivated
   * @type {Array} deactivated features
   */
  deactivate: function deactivate(features) {
    activeFeatures =
      activeFeatures.filter(function (feature) {
        return !contains(features, feature);
      });
    setFlags(activeFeatures);
```

```
            this.emit('deactivated', features);
            return this;
          }
        },

        // Creates the feature toggle object by
        // composing these methods with an
        // event emitter using the Stampit
        // prototypal inheritance library.
        ft = stampit.compose(
          stampit.convertConstructor(EventEmitter),
          stampit(methods)
        ).create();

        // Kick things off by setting feature classes
        // for the currently active features.
        setFlags(activeFeatures);

        return ft;
      };

    module.exports = setFeatures;
```

On the server side, you'll want to check the URL parameters and a features cookie (a saved list of feature overrides), get the list of currently active features from the feature database, and combine that data to calculate the currently active features for the current user.

The list of features sent by the server is often influenced by a number of different criteria. A common example: say you want to roll out a feature to 20% of the users. You can use a clever trick to base the user percentile on the user ID. Of course this won't produce exactly even distributions, but for user communities numbering in the thousands, it's usually a close enough approximation:

```
userPercentage = function userPercentage(userId, percent) {
  var id = parseInt(userId, 36);
  return (id % 100 < percent);
};
```

Other common criteria include whitelisted users and whitelisted user groups, user sign-up date, paid versus unpaid users, andtype of account.

Conclusion

Feature toggles offer tremendous gains in the integration process, allowing companies to ship updates without the nightmare of coordinating a release across many features and teams working on new product features.

They also allow you to test new features in the actual production environment without interfering with the user experience.

Gradual feature rollout allows you to gauge the impact of a change and roll back changes with a minimal impact on user experience and productivity.

As you've seen, it's not hard to integrate feature toggles into your code, and it offers a great deal of value. It's no wonder that feature toggles have been adopted by so many industry-leading software teams.

## CHAPTER 10

Internationalization

When you build a web application that grows to or near the saturation point in one country or culture, the easiest way to grow your user base is to expand to other cultures.

Internationalization or localization is the process of converting text strings, numbers, dates, and currency into localized languages and representations. One of the biggest hurdles to cross is obviously the translation of your app, but before you can even start down that road, you need to have some mechanisms in place to make that possible.

So when is the right time to get started? *Right now.* The biggest obstacle to translation is that you must plan for it or budget a whole lot more time and energy to painstakingly go through the app, find all the strings that need translating, and then add support for it after the fact. By far, the easiest way to support internationalization is to plan for it up front, as soon as you start building templates. Any string that gets displayed to the user should be run through a translation function first.

Instead of rolling your own translation solution, I recommend that you find a library to handle it for you. Some good ones include Moment.js (*http://momentjs.com/*) for dates, and i18next (*http://i18next.com/*) for strings.

Microsoft produced a very thorough solution that works with strings, numbers, currency, percentages, and dates. It's called Globalize (*https://github.com/jquery/globalize*), and it was generously donated to the jQuery project, but it has since been made stand-alone and converted to work with AMD and node-style modules. You don't need to use jQuery to use Globalize.

One advantage of Globalize is that it uses a fairly comprehensive database of locale information that is hard to match in JavaScript. It uses the Unicode Common Locale Data Repository (CLDR) (*http://cldr.unicode.org/*). CLDR is used by many of the top software development companies, including Apple, Google, IBM, and Adobe. Anybody can contribute to it. You could think of it is the Wikipedia of globalization data.

Once you've chosen a solution, getting your translation data where it needs to be is your next challenge. It doesn't make sense to ship the whole catalog of translation data to the client if they only need a single locale set.

If you render all your templates on the client side, you can inject a default set of translations into the page data at page-load time, or make an asynchronous call to fetch translations, or both.

 There have been apps where the page renders, and then an alternate translation loads, and the page re-renders. Those cases can present an awkward user experience, so make sure that you resolve the preferred locale before you invoke your initial page render.

Once it has been determined that the user has a locale preference different from the default, it's important to store that information so that you can present him with his preferred locale experience at every subsequent page load. It's a good idea to set a cookie that contains this information. It's probably not a good idea to store that information in a server-side session, because if the user is not logged in, or the session is expired, the user might have trouble logging in and getting his preferred locale experience back.

Unfortunately, there is no easy way to get a user's true locale preference on the client side without asking. However, the browser's request header can tell you the user's preference. There's a locale module for express that makes the best match easy to get:

```
var locale = require('locale'),
    // ... other requires ...
    // Tell locale which locales you support.
    supportedLocales = ['en', 'en_US', 'ja'];

// locale() returns a middleware function that pulls the
// req.headers["accept-language"] attribute and runs the value
// through locales.best(supported) to determine the closest
// matching locale.
app.use( locale(supportedLocales) );
```

Once you get the user's preference, it's probably a good idea to bundle any required locale data with the same response payload so that you don't incur the latency hit of an extra request. Most libraries will let you load translations from a JSON data object embedded in the page. For example, Globalize includes a `.loadTranslation()` method:

```
Globalize.loadTranslation('pt_BR', {
  greetings: {
    hello: "Olá",
    bye: "Tchau"
  }
});
```

To translate some text:

```
// Set the locale
Globalize.locale('pt_BR');

// Select the text you want to translate.
// Organized by path:
Globalize.translate('greetings/bye');
```

Conclusion

I hope you're thinking of how you can incorporate translations into whatever app you're currently working on. Remember, it's really hard to add translation capabilities to your app after the fact. Get in the habit of running all of your text through a translate function as soon as you start writing your first lines of code. When your app smashes its way through cultural divides, you'll be handsomely rewarded for the little bit of extra effort.

If you're a small developer and you think that translations might be out of your reach, you may be surprised. Services like One Hour Translation (*http://www.onehourtransla tion.com/*) and Tethras (*http://www.tethras.com/*) charge less than $0.20 per word with no minimums. At that rate, you could translate a fairly complex application for just a few hundred dollars.

JavaScript Style Guide

You don't need to know the arcane inner workings of JavaScript in order to do lots of useful things with it. However, if you plan to write an application with tens of thousands of lines of code, you're going to need to explore a little deeper. Here you'll explore some fundamentals that will help you build large applications that are still maintainable. For more on these subjects, I strongly recommend *JavaScript: The Good Parts* by Douglas Crockford.

Example Tests

In the real world, applications are fragile. When you change them, things often break, and you need an easy way to detect those broken things so you can fix them before your users are impacted.

Manual quality assurance is an expensive, time-consuming, and tedious process, and the larger your code base grows, the bigger the job gets. One commonly accepted solution to this problem is to write tests that assure your code does what you expect.

Tests can aid in debugging as well. Frequently when a large number of components interact (often indirectly), it's difficult to tell which component a bug is hiding in. If you have a test suite, and one component breaks, you'll be alerted immediately to which component isn't behaving the way it was designed to behave.

Throughout this book you'll see QUnit tests (*http://docs.jquery.com/QUnit*) in examples to alert you to expected and actual behaviors. QUnit is a JavaScript unit test framework that generates clear, readable test output on whatever page you include it in. It's the test suite used by jQuery (*http://jquery.com/*).

It is safe to assume that all tests pass, unless you see a comment that says otherwise. For example:

```
var highPass = function highPass(number, cutoff) {
  if (number >= cutoff) {
    return true;
  } else {
    return false;
  }
},

lowPass = function lowPass(number, cutoff) {
  if (number >= cutoff) {
    return true;
  } else {
    return false;
  }
};

module('Filter Examples');

test('highPass', function () {
  ok(!highPass(2, 5), 'Lower values should not pass.');
  ok(highPass(8, 5), 'Higher values should pass.');
});

test('lowPass', function () {
  ok(lowPass(2, 5), 'Lower values should pass.'); // Fails
  ok(!lowPass(8, 5),
    'Higher values should not pass.'); // Fails
});
```

The first test passes the tests as written. The second test set fails because the logic needs to be inverted in `lowPass()`:

```
if (number >= cutoff) {
```

becomes:

```
if (number <= cutoff) {
```

QUnit Primer

This book demonstrates several QUnit functions:

- `module()`
- `test()`
- `ok()`
- `equal()`

The `module()` function allows you to group related functionality in your test output. The `name` parameter can be any string:

```
module( 'Name');
```

The `test()` function lets you name and define individual module tests. All assertions go inside tests:

```
test('Name', function () {
  // Your assertions here...
});
```

You can test the truthiness of an expression with `ok()`:

```
ok(true, 'Description');
```

The first parameter can be any expression you wish to evaluate. If the expression is truthy, the assertion will pass. You can do anything you want with the description, but I like to write them like: *Subject* should *verb*. For example, "User should exist," "Valid input should pass," etc. If you find yourself writing "*Subject* should *be...*" consider using `equal()` instead.

The `equal()` function allows you to compare the equality of two values. For example:

```
var a = true;

equal(a, true, 'a should be true.');
```

Code Quality

When you approach JavaScript for application development, style becomes more important than it is in the context of one-off scripts. Code is more readable if code style and conventions are used consistently. That's not to say that your style shouldn't evolve as you hone your skills: rather, it should converge on a set of standards that other developers can learn and use.

Some style choices are arbitrary, but many best practices have emerged in the JavaScript community. In this section, we'll cover a few of the more important style considerations you should be aware of.

Perhaps the easiest way to start converging on a code quality standard is to begin *linting* your code with a tool like *JSLint*. Linters scan your source code for syntax errors (and in the case of JSLint, some stylistic errors, as well).

The most obvious reason to use a lint tool is that it can be an extremely valuable debugging asset. Most bugs are the result of syntax errors. If a tool can help you eliminate all syntax-related bugs from your code quickly, you'll see huge gains in productivity.

A few of the style choices enforced in JSLint have raised controversy in the JavaScript community, but even if you don't agree with every point that the author, Douglas Crockford (*http://www.crockford.com/*), makes about JavaScript style, it's important to have a thorough understanding of why those choices were made.

More importantly, using an automated tool like JSLint is the best way to enforce a minimum level of code quality and style throughout the code base. In my experience, getting all the developers on the same page is worth a little sacrifice in style.

If you can make the trade-offs, what you gain in increased productivity is extraordinary. However, if you can't make one or two of the trade-offs prescribed by JSLint, there is a tool for you, as well: JSHint. In JSHint, the rules are more flexible.

 Think carefully before choosing to ignore the recommendations of JSLint. While some of them may seem arbitrary at first, they're all there for a reason.

Best Practices Quick Reference

Any time somebody starts dictating style, there is an inevitable backlash. Douglas Crockford is famously unapologetic about the style dictation enforced by JSLint and firmly believes that everybody should be using it as he prefers to have it configured. I have a lot of respect for the work that he put into it, but my view on style is a bit more flexible.

Some of the recommendations here are more important than others, but all of them are about improving the quality and consistency of your code. As you learn new things over the years, you should learn better ways to accomplish those goals. This section is not meant to be taken as gospel. Instead, it's meant to get you thinking and help you understand ways that you can improve the overall quality of the code you write. If your style never deviates from the style I recommend in this book, I believe that would be unfortunate. I don't want to see JavaScript style stagnate; I want to see it improve over time as we learn new things as a community.

Indentation: Be Consistent

Tabs or spaces? It's common for people to have very strong feelings, but both have their merits. Tab users say it saves them keystrokes, there are never any hidden whitespace characters, and tabs allow users to set their own indentation display preferences. Space users say that most editors will automatically substitute spaces for tabs and support "soft tabs" that have similar display characteristics to tabs. And you can line up your code better with more fine-grained control of your whitespace. All good points. Too close to call a clear winner.

What's important is that you pick one and stick with it. If you're working as a team, all members of the team should use the same standard.

Use Semicolons

There is a recent and growing movement in JavaScript circles to use a style that leaves off optional semicolons. When the JavaScript runtime encounters a condition where there should be a semicolon to make sense of the code but can't find one, it inserts a semicolon automatically. This behavior is called automatic semicolon insertion (ASI).

The new style depends on ASI to produce valid JavaScript code for the engine to execute. In my opinion, this style should be avoided in the short term but maybe embraced in the long term.

The problem with the new style is not in the style itself. Provided you follow a few simple rules, it is a readable and viable. Less syntax is sometimes more.

The problem is that there are currently no automated lint tools that I am aware of which can ignore your missing semicolons when they're not required but highlight the error cases where leaving out the semicolon will cause ambiguities that ASI can't resolve. Lint tools are highly valuable, and missing semicolons are among the most common sources of bugs. I can't recommend a style that would require you to abandon useful lint rules.

Whatever you do, don't just leave all semicolons out. Sometimes, semicolons are required. The following tests all fail due to missing semicolons:

```
test('Missing semicolon before +', function () {
  var a = 1 + 1
    +'3';

  equal(a, 2,
    'a should be 2.'
  ); // Fails. a = 23
});

test('Missing semicolon before [', function () {
  var b = 1 + 1
  [1, 1].forEach(function (num) {
    b += num;
  });

  // Error: Cannot call method forEach of undefined.
  equal(b, 4,
    'b should be 4.');
});

test('Missing semicolon before (', function () {
  var x = 1,
    f = function f () {
      ok(false, 'This test should not run.'); // Fails.
    }

  (function () {
    /* Do something interesting. */
```

```
      }());
    });
```

Bracket Placement: Right Side

Due to automatic semicolon insertion, brackets should always be placed to the right, on the line that begins the statement in the first getLocation().

Wrong:

```
var getLocation = function getLocation()
{
  return
  {
    x: 20,
    y: 20
  };
};
```

Right:

```
var getLocation = function getLocation() {
  return {
    x: 20,
    y: 20
  };
};
```

Avoid Name Collisions

The default scope for variables in JavaScript is global. Every other script on the page has to share that namespace. In order to prevent name collisions, your application should use as few global names as possible. Typically, that would be a single name for the application and possibly a handful of others for supporting libraries, such as jQuery and Underscore.

Wrong: x is global:

```
var x;
// Do stuff with x...
```

Right: x is local to the wrapping function:

```
(function myScript() {
  var x;
  // Do stuff with x...
}());
```

This type of function wrapper is called an Immediately Invoked Function Expression (IIFE, pronounced "iffy"). For details, see "Immediately Invoked Function Expressions" on page 18.

Modules are the best way to avoid name collisions in JavaScript. See Chapter 4. The preceding code is an example of the module pattern described in the modules chapter, but there are several other types of modules, including AMD and Node-style modules.

Always Use var

If you forget to use the var keyword, your variable assignments will pollute the global scope.

Wrong: x is global:

```
var add = function add(number) {
  x = 2;
  return number + x;
  };

test('Without var.', function () {
  equal(add(2), 4,
    'add() should add 2 to whatever you pass in.');

  // Fails
  ok(!x, 'x should not pollute the global scope.');
});
```

Right: function scope:

```
var add = function add(number) {
  var x = 2;
  return number + x;
};

test('With var.', function () {
  equal(add(2), 4,
    'add() should add 2 to whatever you pass in.');

  ok(!x, 'x should not pollute the global scope.');
});
```

Use One var Statement per Function

Because of the peculiarities with hoisting (see "Hoisting" on page 22), you should only use one var statement per function, at the top of your function. Some style guides disagree with me on this, but in practice, every time I see multiple var statements used as a matter of style on a team with several developers, variable declarations tend to slip down away from the top of the function, which opens the door to hoisting bugs.

Wrong: multiple var statements:

```
(function myScript() {
  var x = true;
  var y = true;
```

```
    /* do some stuff with x and y */
    var z = true;
    /* do some stuff with z */
}());
```

Right: one `var` per function:

```
(function myScript() {
    var x = true,
    y = true,
    z = true;
    /* do some stuff with x, y, and z */
}());
```

Avoid Constant Abuse

Constants are a class of types that allow you to specify names for values that never change. They're used to express things like mathematical constants (like pi), fixed ratios (the number of seconds in a minute), etc. If a constant is able to change, it will likely break the code that relies on it. It is for this reason that in most languages, constants are immutable.

That is not the case in JavaScript. There is a `const` keyword coming to JavaScript, but it will likely be a few years before you can safely use it for cross-browser code. This hasn't stopped people from faking constants in JavaScript, however.

The general convention is to use all caps to name constants. This convention is much older than JavaScript, and the well-understood meaning is, "You can count on this value to never change, and to never need changing." Because you can't count on fake constants to be constant, it's probably better not to fake it at all. If you really need the value to be safe, store it in a closure and use a getter function to access it. See "Closures" on page 25.

More often than not in practice, I've seen fake constants abused for things that never should have been considered constant in the first place. It's very common to confuse constants and configuration.

Code that employs constants instead of configuration tends to get more rigid and brittle as it grows. If you can't configure a module, the same code tends to get rewritten with few differences, except for variable names and a few differences in constant declarations.

Employing configuration instead of constants allows you to reuse the code, instead of writing new code.

Wrong: abusing constants:

```
var createUserBox = function createUserBox() {
    var WIDTH = '80px',
        HEIGHT = '80px';

    return {
```

```
        width: WIDTH,
        height: HEIGHT
      };
    },

  createMenuBox = function createMenuBox() {
    var WIDTH = '200px',
    HEIGHT = '400px';

    return {
      width: WIDTH,
      height: HEIGHT
    };
  };

test('Avoid Constants', function () {
  var userBox = createUserBox(),
    menuBox = createMenuBox();

  equal(userBox.width, '80px',
    'userBox should be 80px wide.');

  equal(menuBox.width, '200px',
    'menuBox should be 200px wide.');
});
```

Right: favor configuration:

```
var createBox = function createBox(options) {
  var defaults = {
    width: '80px',
    height: '80px'
  };

  return $.extend({}, defaults, options);
};

test('Avoid Constants', function () {
  var userBox = createBox({
    width: '80px',
    height: '80px'
  }),

  menuBox = createBox({
    width: '200px',
    height: '400px'
  });

  equal(userBox.width, '80px',
    'userBox should be 80px wide.');

  equal(menuBox.width, '200px',
```

```
      'menuBox should be 200px wide.');
  });
```

Use Functional Iterators When Possible

JavaScript offers the capability to program in a functional style, meaning that you can pass functions as arguments to other functions and apply the passed in function to each element in a data resource (array or object). The technique is handy because it can make your code more readable, abstract away the looping mechanics, and keep the loop control variables isolated from your main function. That said, loops can give you finer-grained control, and there can be performance considerations when you're looping over very large datasets.

Good:

```
var getCount = function getCount() {
  var i,
    count = [1, 2, 3],
    length = count.length,
    text = '';

  for (i = 0; i < length; i += 1) {
    text += count[i] + ' ';
  }

  return text;
};

test('Looping over an array:', function () {
  var text = getCount();

  equal(text, '1 2 3 ',
    'getCount() should count to three.');
});
```

Better for most situations:

```
var getCount = function getCount() {
  var count = [1, 2, 3],
    text = '';

  count.forEach(function (number) {
    text += number + ' ';
  });

  return text;
};

test('Functional iterator:', function () {
  var text = getCount();

  equal(text, '1 2 3 ',
```

```
      'getCount() should count to three.'
    );
  });
```

Note that you don't need to worry about the `i` or `length` variables in this version.

Even better: use the right utility for the job, and you can eliminate even more variables and avoid mutating variables outside the lambda:

```
var getCount = function getCount() {
  var count = [1, 2, 3];

  return count.reduce(function (previous, number) {
    return previous + number + ' ';
  }, '');
};
```

Functional iterators were added in ECMAScript 5, meaning that you'll need to shim them to prevent throwing errors in older browsers. Here's the MDN `.forEach()` shim:

```
// Shim .forEach()
if ( !Array.prototype.forEach ) {
  Array.prototype.forEach = function(fn, scope) {
    for (var i = 0, len = this.length; i < len; ++i) {
      fn.call(scope || this, this[i], i, this);
    }
  };
}
```

A *shim* is any code that wraps a standard API call in order to abstract it. Shims can be used to normalize cross-browser behavior. A *polyfill* is a shim that implements new standard features from JavaScript, HTML5, and related technologies using existing capabilities in order to deliver that new functionality to older browsers. To learn more about using JavaScript polyfills, search for any new feature in the JavaScript method descriptions on the *Mozilla Developer Network* (MDN). Most of the new features include a complete or partial polyfill in the description. If you want to make it really easy, try the ES5-shim project (*https://github.com/es-shims/es5-shim*).

The MDN documentation is perhaps the most thorough and authoritative online JavaScript reference. If you add the keyword "MDN" when you search Google for JavaScript features, it should pull up the MDN documentation instead of other much less reliable and much less complete references online.

Be Careful with if Statements

The results of type coercion in JavaScript can be difficult to predict, even when you know the rules. Here you'll see how subtle differences in comparisons can lead to significant changes in the results.

Be careful when relying on truthiness for logic. Whenever possible, use comparison operators to clarify your meaning. Falsy values include:

- `0`
- `undefined`
- `null`
- empty strings
- `false`

 Boolean objects instantiated with `new Boolean(false)` are *truthy* because they're objects, and objects are truthy. In order to test against them you need to use the `.valueOf()` method. It's better to use `true` and `false` instead.

Empty objects and empty arrays are truthy, including objects created with `new Boolean(false)`.

Wrong: don't use `new Boolean()`:

```
var myBool = new Boolean(false);

test('Boolean object', function () {
  ok(!myBool, 'Should be falsy'); // Fails

  ok(!myBool.valueOf(),
  'Should be falsy.'); // Passes
});
```

Right: use `true` or `false` in your boolean declarations:

```
var myBool = false;

test('Boolean object', function () {
  ok(!myBool, '!myBool should be false.');
});
```

The following series of tests are meant to demonstrate how different types of comparisons in JavaScript that look similar can deliver very different results. Always be careful that you're using the correct test for your situation:

```
function truthy(x) {
  if (x) {
    return true;
  } else {
    return false;
  }
}

test('Truthy', function () {
  // Falsy
  equal(truthy(0), true, 'truthy(0)'); // Fail
  equal(truthy(''), true, "truthy('')"); // Fail
  equal(truthy(null), true, 'truthy(null)'); // Fail
  equal(truthy(undefined), true,
  'truthy(undefined)'); // Fail
  equal(truthy(false), true, 'truthy(false)'); // Fail

  // Truthy
  equal(truthy('0'), true, "truthy('0')"); // Pass
  equal(truthy(new Boolean(false)), true,
  'truthy(new Boolean(false))'); // Pass
  equal(truthy({}), true, 'truthy({})'); // Pass
  equal(truthy([]), true, 'truthy([])'); // Pass
  equal(truthy([0]), true, 'truthy([0])'); // Pass
  equal(truthy([1]), true, 'truthy([1])'); // Pass
  equal(truthy(['0']), true, "truthy(['0'])"); // Pass
  equal(truthy(['1']), true, "truthy(['1'])"); // Pass
});
```

These are the falsy and truthy values we'll use as a baseline for a series of other comparisons.

 Often, developers will use if (x) when they really want to see if the value has been set at all. This is especially problematic when 0, empty strings, or false are valid values. In that case, you want the test to pass as long as the expression evaluates to anything other than null or undefined. A good rule of thumb is to only use if (x) to evaluate booleans or the existence of objects or arrays.

```
function exists(x) {
  if (x !== undefined && x !== null) {
    return true;
  } else {
    return false;
  }
}

test('exists', function () {
  // Falsy
  equal(exists(0), true, 'exists(0)'); // Pass
```

```
      equal(exists(''), true, "exists('')"); // Pass
      equal(exists(null), true, 'exists(null)');
      equal(exists(undefined), true, 'exists(undefined)');
      equal(exists(false), true, 'exists(false)'); // Pass

      // Truthy
      equal(exists('0'), true, "exists('0')"); // Pass
      equal(exists(new Boolean(false)), true,
      'exists(new Boolean(false))'); // Pass
      equal(exists({}), true, 'exists({})'); // Pass
      equal(exists([]), true, 'exists([])'); // Pass
      equal(exists([0]), true, 'exists([0])'); // Pass
      equal(exists([1]), true, 'exists([1])'); // Pass
      equal(exists(['0']), true, "exists(['0'])"); // Pass
      equal(exists(['1']), true, "exists(['1'])"); // Pass
    });
```

Of course, a shorter version of that function will return the same results:

```
function exists(x) {
  return (x !== undefined && x !== null);
}
```

 The == operator can return some problematic results due to type coercion. For example, say you're checking an array to be sure it contains a valid price, and some items cost $0.00. Your code could fail because ['0.00'] == false. Use === instead.

```
var isFalse = function isFalse(x) {
  return (x == false);
};

test('isFalse using ==', function () {
  // Falsy
  equal(isFalse(0), true, 'isFalse(0)'); // Pass
  equal(isFalse(''), true, "isFalse('')"); // Pass
  equal(isFalse(null), true, 'isFalse(null)'); // Fail
  equal(isFalse(undefined), true, 'isFalse(undefined)'); // Fail
  equal(isFalse(false), true, 'isFalse(false)'); // Pass


  // Truthy
  equal(isFalse('0'), true, "isFalse('0')"); // Pass
  equal(isFalse(new Boolean(false)), true,
  'isFalse(new Boolean(false))'); // Pass
  equal(isFalse({}), true, 'isFalse({})'); // Fail
  equal(isFalse([]), true, 'isFalse([])'); // Pass
  equal(isFalse([0]), true, 'isFalse([0])'); // Pass
  equal(isFalse([1]), true, 'isFalse([1])'); // Fail
  equal(isFalse(['0']), true, "isFalse(['0'])"); // Pass
```

```
  equal(isFalse(['1']), true, "isFalse(['1'])"); // Fail
});
```

The following code will only return true if x is actually set to false:

```
var isFalse = function isFalse(x) {
  return (x === false);
};
```

The following function is dangerous, because it will return true for 1, [1], and ['1']:

```
var isTrue = function isTrue(x) {
  return (x == true);
};
```

Use === instead to eliminate the possibility of false positives.

Remember that if (x) will always return true when x is an object—even if the object is empty. It's common to use *ducktyping* when you examine objects. (If it walks like a duck and talks like a duck, treat it like a duck.) The idea is similar to using feature detection in browsers instead of running checks against the browser string. Ducktyping is feature detection for objects:

```
if (typeof foo.bar === 'function') {
  foo.bar();
}
```

Avoid Side Effects

In order to avoid unintended side effects, only assign to variables declared inside your function, or declared as formal parameters. See "Minimize Side Effects" on page 10.

Wrong: has side effects:

```
var x = 0;

function increment() {
  x += 1;
  return x;
}

test('increment() with side effects.', function () {
  var val = increment();

  equal(val, 1,
    'increment() should add one.'
  );

  equal(x, 0,
    'x should be unchanged outside the function.'
  ); // Fails
});
```

Right: no side effects:

```
var x = 0;

function increment(x) {
  x += 1;
  return x;
}

test('increment() without side effects.', function () {
  var val = increment(x);

  equal(val, 1,
    'increment() adds one.');

  equal(x, 0,
    'x is unchanged.');
});
```

Wherever possible, you should avoid mutating objects declared outside your function. This isn't always practical, but where it is, your code will be more reusable and less *brittle* (likely to break when unrelated code changes).

Use with caution: object-mutation side effects:

```
var obj = {
    value: 2
  };

function setValue(obj, value) {
  obj.value = value;
  return obj;
}

test('setValue() with side effects', function () {
  var myObj = setValue(obj, 3);

  equal(myObj.value, 3,
    'setValue() returns new value.');

  equal(obj.value, 2,
    'The original should be unchanged.'
  ); // Fails
});
```

Better: return a new object:

```
var obj = {
    value: 2
  };

function setValue(obj, value) {
  // Note: extend() is jQuery.extend(),
```

```
  // Underscore .extend(), or similar...
  var instance = extend({}, obj);

  return instance;
}

test('setValue() without side effects', function () {
  var myObj = setValue(obj, 3);

  equal(myObj.value, 3,
    'setValue() should return new value.');

  equal(obj.value, 2,
    'The original is should be unchanged!'); // Passes
});
```

Don't Use switch

JavaScript has pretty normal control-flow statements that use blocks delineated by curly braces. There is an exception to this: the switch ... case statement. The strange thing about switch ... case is that you must include the keyword break at the end of each case to prevent control from falling through to the next case. *Fall through* is a trick that allows you to let more than one case be executed. Control will fall through automatically to the next case unless you explicitly tell it not to with break. However, like the optional semicolons and curly braces, it's possible to forget break when you really should have used it. When that happens, the bug is difficult to find because the code *looks correct*. For that reason, the break statement should never be left off of a case, even by design.

With that said, JavaScript has an elegant object-literal syntax and first-class functions, which makes it simple to create a keyed *method lookup*. The object you create for your method lookup is called an *action object* or *command object* and is used in many software *design patterns*.

Say you're creating a game where the nonplayer fight actions are selected based on an algorithm defined elsewhere and passed in to doAction as a string. The switch ... case form looks like this:

```
function doAction(action) {
  switch (action) {
    case 'hack':
      return 'hack';
    break;

    case 'slash':
      return 'slash';
    break;

    case 'run':
      return 'run';
```

```
      break;

    default:
      throw new Error('Invalid action.');
      break;
  }
}
```

The method lookup version looks like this:

```
function doAction(action) {
  var actions = {
    'hack': function () {
      return 'hack';
    },

    'slash': function () {
      return 'slash';
    },

    'run': function () {
      return 'run';
    }
  };

  if (typeof actions[action] !== 'function') {
    throw new Error('Invalid action.');
  }


  return actions[action]();
}
```

Or, for input grouping (a frequent use case for the fall-through feature): say you're writing a programming language parser, and you want to perform one action whenever you encounter a *token* that opens an object or array, and another whenever you encounter a token that closes them. Assume the following functions exist:

```
function handleOpen(token) {
  return 'Open object / array.';
}

function handleClose(token) {
  return 'Close object / array';
}
```

The switch ... case form is:

```
function processToken (token) {
  switch (token) {
    case '{':
    case '[':
      handleOpen(token);
```

```
    break;

  case ']':
  case '}':
    handleClose(token);
    break;

  default:
    throw new Error('Invalid token.');
    break;
  }
}
```

The method lookup version looks like this:

```
var tokenActions = {
    '{': handleOpen,
    '[': handleOpen,
    ']': handleClose,
    '}': handleClose
  };

function processToken(token) {
  if (typeof tokenActions[token] !== 'function') {
    throw new Error('Invalid token.');
  }

  return tokenActions[token](token);
}
```

At first glance, it might seem like this is more complicated syntax, but it has a few advantages:

- It uses the standard curly-bracket blocks used everywhere else in JavaScript.

- You never have to worry about remembering the `break`.

- Method lookup is much more flexible. Using an action object allows you to alter the cases dynamically at runtime, for example, to allow dynamically loaded modules to extend cases, or even swap out some or all of the cases for modal context switching.

- Method lookup is object oriented by definition. With `switch ... case`, your code is more procedural.

The last point is perhaps the most important. The `switch` statement is a close relative of the `goto` statement, which computer scientists argued for 20 years to eradicate from modern programming languages. It has the same serious drawback: almost everywhere I've seen `switch ... case` used, I've seen it abused. Developers group unrelated functionality into overly-clever branching logic. In other words, `switch ... case` tends to encourage *spaghetti code*, while method lookup tends to encourage well-organized, object-oriented code. It's far too common to find implementations of switch ... case, which violate the principles of *high cohesion* and *separation of concerns*.

I was once a fan of switch ... case as a better alternative to if ... else, but after becoming more familiar with JavaScript, I naturally fell into using method lookup instead. I haven't used switch ... case in my code for several years. I don't miss it at all.

If you ever find yourself writing a switch statement, stop and ask yourself the following questions:

- Will you ever need to add more cases? (queue, stack, plug-in architecture)
- Would it be useful to modify the list of cases at runtime, for example, to change the list of enabled options based on context? (mode switching)
- Would it be useful to log the cases that get executed, for example, to create an undo/ redo stack, or log user actions to your servers for analysis? (*command manager*)
- Are you referencing your cases by incrementing numbers, for example, case 1:, case: 2, etc.? (*iterator* target)
- Are you trying to group related inputs together with the fall through feature so that they can share code?

If you answered yes to any of these questions, there is almost certainly a better implementation that doesn't utilize switch or its slippery fall-through feature.

Don't Use eval()

The desire to use eval() should be considered a *code smell* (as in, "something smells fishy"). It's a good indication that there is probably a better way to accomplish what you're after.

 You'll often hear programmers say things like, "this smells," or "something smells funny here." They're not talking about the garlic burger you had for lunch; they're expressing that something doesn't feel right about the code. Maybe a function is too long, or it's doing too much. Maybe there's a better, smarter, faster, or easier way to accomplish the same goal. Things like large inheritance trees and deeply nested logic send up red flags for experienced programmers. Those are code smells.

JavaScript is a very flexible, expressive, dynamic language with a lot less need for eval() than most other languages.

Most of what eval() can do for you can be done with code that is faster and easier to read. Using eval() forces the JavaScript engine to delay compilation of the eval() code, bypassing the usual code compilation flow and hindering compiler optimizations.

eval() can also poke holes in your security and allow cross-site scripting (XSS) attacks.

Some good alternatives to eval() and its dopplegangers include square bracket notation and runtime object mutation. The eval() function should only be used with great caution, and only if it is absolutely the only way to accomplish your goal.

eval() is also prohibited in many places where application security is a concern. For instance, eval() is not allowed in Chrome extensions (*https://developer.chrome.com/extensions/sandboxingEval*) unless it's sandboxed.

The eval() function has dopplegangers you should also avoid:

- Passing a string to the Function() constructor
- Passing a string value to setTimeout() or setInterval() (as opposed to a function reference or lambda expression)

Index

Symbols

() (parentheses), 20

A

acceptance criteria, 87
access control
    about, 137
    authentication, 137–147
    authorization, 147–150
    recommendations, 150
access control lists (ACLs), 147
ACLs (access control lists), 147
ad-hoc polymorphism, 32
.addEventListener() method, 22
.addTo() function, 17
affordances (hypermedia), 182
agile development methods, 87
Ajax technology, 2, 42
alerts, logging, 165
Alman, Ben, 18
Amazon Simple Queue Service (SQS), 108
AMD (asynchronous module definition)
    about, 79–80
    exporting, 188
    loader plug-ins, 81–82
Amundsen, Mike, 182
Angular library, 114

anonymous functions
    about, 13–15
    self-invoked, 18
AppDynamics tool, 166
application development
    bundling and deployment, 93–97
    code quality, 209
    defining the app, 87–90
    feature implementation, 90–92
args array, 30
arguments object, 29
arity (functions), 28
Armstrong, Joe, 49
array literal notation, 52
Array.prototype.shift() method, 30
Array.prototype.slice() method, 30
Array.sort() method, 37
arrays
    as collections, 33
    as objects, 47
The Art of Agile Development (Shore), 87
ASI (automatic semicolon insertion), 211
aspect-oriented programming, 101
asynchronous module definition (AMD)
    about, 79–80
    exporting, 188
    loader plug-ins, 81–82
asynchronous operations
    about, 41

We'd like to hear your suggestions for improving our indexes. Send email to index@oreilly.com.

invoking, 20
JavaScript advantages, 3
JSON and, 6
lambdas, 16–18, 52
method design, 27–36
minimizing side effects, 10–12
as objects, 47
polymorphic, 29–32
sorting parameters, 30

G

Gamma, Erich, viii, 77
Gang of Four, viii, 48–50, 73
gconf package, 129
generic programming, 32–34
geofencing, 144
Geolocation API (HTML), 144
GET verb (HTTP), 7, 159, 163, 175, 178
Globalize plug-in (Microsoft), 203
Goodman, Danny, 106
Google Analytics, 166–168
Google Authenticator, 143
Google Instant, 3
gorilla/banana problem, 49
Grunt task runner, 93–96, 122

H

H-Factors, 182
HAProxy module, 191
HATEOAS acronym, 183–184
Helm, Richard, viii
Hickson, Ian, 124
higher order functions, 3, 18
hoisting (function scope), 22–25
HTML
    as API media type, 185
    Geolocation API, 144
HTTP verbs
    logging requests, 159
    RESTful APIs and, 7–8, 175, 178
hypermedia
    about, 182
    affordances and, 182
    HATEOAS acronym and, 183–184
    HTML and, 185
    Jade template engine, 185–187
    Jiron type, 187–189

I

i18next library, 203
IcoMoon app, 97
if statement, 218–221
IIFE (immediately invoked function expression), 18–20, 77
immediately invoked function expression (IIFE), 18–20, 77
import keyword, 86
indentation (best practice), 210
infrastructure diagram, 4–5
inherence factor (authentication), 144
inheritance
    classical, 3, 48–50
    problems caused by, 49
    prototypal, 2, 51, 64–69, 123
interfaces in modular design, 73–77
internalization process, 203–205

J

Jade template engine, 185–187
Januska, Antonin, 89
JavaScript
    about, 1
    advantages of, 2–4
    anatomy of modern apps, 4–8
    best practices reference, 210–227
    code quality, 209
    example tests, 207
    fluent style, 51–53
JavaScript Object Notation (JSON)
    about, 2
    data storage and communication, 5–6
    Jiron comparison, 188
    RESTful web services and, 6–8
JavaScript: The Definitive Guide (Flannagan), viii
JavaScript: The Good Parts (Crockford), viii, 207
Jiron hypermedia type, 187–189
Johnson, Ralph, viii
jQuery
    .on() method, 41
    AMD support, 80
    collection polymorphism and, 34
    dynamic dispatch and, 32
    .extend() method, 29, 56, 76
    fluent APIs, 35–36

building client-side code, 87–97
design principles, 72
ES6, 86
interfaces and, 73–77
managing, 102–105
module pattern, 77–79
node style, 82–83
npm support, 84–86
separation of concerns, 99
Moment.js library, 203
MongoDB data stores, 6
Monthly Recurring Revenue (MRR), 154
Mozilla Developer Network (MDN), 217
Mozilla Persona, 145
MRR (Monthly Recurring Revenue), 154
multifactor authentication
about, 143
inherence factor, 144
knowledge factor, 143
possession factor, 143
MVC (Model View Controller), 114–117
MVP (Model View Presenter), 115

N

name collisions (best practice), 212
named function expressions, 14–16
named parameters (methods), 28
namespaces
best practices, 212
common mistakes, 78
this keyword and, 20, 51
new keyword, 51, 54
New Relic tool, 166, 191
Node environment
about, 125–126, 133
configuration considerations, 128
installing, 126
libraries supported, 128
organizing files in, 127
node package manager (npm), 84–86
Node Version Manager (nvm), 126
Node.js
performance advantages, 2
random generators, 139
Stampit and, 69
Nodetime tool, 167
NoSQL data stores, 5, 6
npm (node package manager), 84–86
nvm (Node Version Manager), 126

O

OAuth 2.0 standard, 149
Object constructor
assign() method, 56
create() method, 53–55, 64, 66, 77
prototype property, 53–55
object literal notation
about, 52
JSON and, 2, 3, 5
object creation example, 60
object-oriented design
foundational principles, 48
gorilla/banana problem, 49
on inheritance, 49–50
objects
about, 47
as collections, 33
creating, 59–61, 65–69
factory methods, 52, 61–64
fluent APIs and, 36
fluent style JavaScript and, 51–53
JavaScript advantages, 2
promises and deferreds, 42–44
prototypal inheritance, 3, 51, 64–69
prototypes, 52–59
ok() function, 209
One Hour Translation service, 205
one-time passwords (OTPs), 143
Open Closed Principle, 72
OpenID, 145, 149
optimizing for speed (design principle), 191
Osmani, Addy, 102
OTPs (one-time passwords), 143

P

parameters
named, 28
sorting, 30
parametric polymorphism, 32
parentheses (), 20
partial application, 40
password salts, 138
passwords
about, 137
brute force attacks, 139–140
password salts, 138
rainbow tables, 138
stolen, 141

About the Author

Eric Elliott is a veteran of JavaScript application development. He has served as computer scientist for the Adobe Creative Cloud team, JavaScript lead at Tout (social video), head of client-side architecture at Zumba Fitness (the leading global fitness brand), author, public speaker, UX consultant, and viral-application consultant. He lives in the San Francisco Bay Area with the most beautiful woman in the world.

Colophon

The animal on the cover of *Programming JavaScript Applications* is an argali (*Ovis ammon*), a wild sheep that roams the highlands of Central Asia. Argali usually inhabit high altitude regions, about 3,000 to 5,000 meters, but their habitat varies according to geographic location (including mountains, steppe valleys and rocky outcrops, and open desert).

Argali are related to the universally known domestic sheep. They are approximately the same length as domestic sheep, but are much taller and heavier. The general coloration varies between each animal, from light yellow to reddish-brown to dark gray-brown.

Argali are highly gregarious animals, found in large single-sex herds that may number up to 100 individuals. During the mating season, these herds come together and males will compete for access to females. These are often violent competitions and the clashing of horns can be heard reverberating around the mountains.

Although both sexes have horns, those of the male are much larger and more impressive; they can be up to 13 percent of the males' body mass. The corkscrew horns wind forward and are of a formidable weight.

Argali are considered an endangered or threatened species throughout their entire range, due largely to habitat loss from overgrazing of domestic sheep and hunting. As the world's largest sheep, there is a strong lure to gather a trophy specimen. They are hunted for both their meat and their horns, used in traditional Chinese medicine, and poaching continues to be a major problem.

The cover image is from Johnson's Natural History. The cover fonts are URW Typewriter and Guardian Sans. The text font is Adobe Minion Pro; the heading font is Adobe Myriad Condensed; and the code font is Dalton Maag's Ubuntu Mono.

Have it your way.

Get even more for your money.

Join the O'Reilly Community, and register the O'Reilly books you own. It's free, and you'll get:

- $4.99 ebook upgrade offer
- 40% upgrade offer on O'Reilly print books
- Membership discounts on books and events
- Free lifetime updates to ebooks and videos
- Multiple ebook formats, DRM FREE
- Participation in the O'Reilly community
- Newsletters
- Account management
- 100% Satisfaction Guarantee

Signing up is easy:

1. Go to: oreilly.com/go/register
2. Create an O'Reilly login.
3. Provide your address.
4. Register your books.

Note: English-language books only

To order books online:
oreilly.com/store

For questions about products or an order:
orders@oreilly.com

To sign up to get topic-specific email announcements and/or news about upcoming books, conferences, special offers, and new technologies:
elists@oreilly.com

For technical questions about book content:
booktech@oreilly.com

To submit new book proposals to our editors:
proposals@oreilly.com

O'Reilly books are available in multiple DRM-free ebook formats. For more information:
oreilly.com/ebooks

O'REILLY®

CPSIA information can be obtained at www.ICGtesting.com
Printed in the USA
BVOW09s1146160915

418277BV00009B/85/P